TEACH YOURSELF BOOKS

ASTROLOGY

NTC Publishing Group

TO

all serious students
of astrology

TEACH YOURSELF BOOKS

ASTROLOGY

Jeff Mayo

D.M.S.Astrol.(Hon.), F.R.Met. S., D.F.Astrol.S.
Principal-Emeritus, The Mayo School of Astrology

 NTC Publishing Group

Long-renowned as *the* authoritative source for self-guided
learning – with more than 30 million copies sold worldwide –
the *Teach Yourself* series includes over 200 titles in the fields
of languages, crafts, hobbies, sports, and other leisure activities.

This edition was first published in 1992 by NTC Publishing Group,
4255 West Touhy Avenue, Lincolnwood (Chicago), Illinois 60646 –
1975 U.S.A. Originally published by Hodder and Stoughton Ltd.
Copyright 1964 by Jeff Mayo.

Library of Congress Catalog Card Number: 92–80859

Printed in England by Clays Ltd, St Ives plc.

Contents

Appendices

Introduction

Astrology as a subject has survived thousands of years. Today it is emerging from a 'dark period' of several centuries, during which its truths were scorned as mere superstition as man's increasing scientific knowledge developed parallel with an increasing materialistic evaluation of life. During this period the charlatans and fortune-tellers debased and misinterpreted a great truth.

The profound – perhaps, even astounding – truth about astrology is that through its basic formulae one can learn the intricate psychological structure of one's own being; trace the deep-rooted drives and motives for behaving as one does. Its value to parents, social welfare and probation officers, teachers, psychologists, the medical profession, in fact to all who seek truth and understanding of the human mind, is inestimable.

After over thirty years as an astrological-consultant, and teacher of astrology to students in about one hundred and fifty countries, I have yet to meet one who, having put astrology to the test, has rejected the subject as nonsense.

Some readers will quickly learn the subject; for many it will not be easy. I would suggest that you first read through the book, then begin to study, chapter by chapter.

Foreword

It is quite unique for an astrology book to be so continuously successful year after year for 28 years. As its author, one of the greatest rewards is knowing that this little book has introduced thousands of readers to this exciting and profoundly beneficial subject.

When my book was first published in 1964 it was impossible to get a serious discussion of astrology presented on television and in national newspapers. Today, although there is still considerable prejudice by those in the media who have never studied the subject, the relevance of astrology to everyday life is becoming much more widely accepted.

Probably the biggest headline and most exciting breakthrough for astrology in 1977 was the world-wide reporting of the successful astrological research jointly undertaken by Professor Eysenck of the Institute of Psychiatry in London and myself, which is the subject of Chapter 18.

My *Extraversion-Introversion and Sun-sign* research continues to stimulate interest – and sometimes antagonism! – in academic psychological circles. One of the latest studies to replicate my research was by Rooij, Brak and Commandeur of the Department of Psychology at the University of Leiden, the Netherlands, who stated: 'We successfully replicated the result found by Mayo et al. (1978) that persons born with the sun in an odd sign of the zodiac tend to be extraverted, and that persons born with the sun in an even sign tend to be introverted.'

Jeff Mayo
1992

Whatever is born or done this moment of
time, has the qualities of this moment
of time.

DR CARL JUNG

Astrology is assured of recognition from
psychology without further restrictions,
because astrology represents the
summation of all the psychological
knowledge of antiquity.

DR CARL JUNG

From *The Secret of the Golden Flower*,
by Wilhelm and Jung

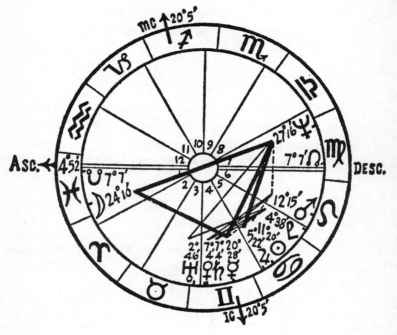

FIGURE 1

Linda
Born 0.34 a.m.
4th July 1942
Windsor, England

What is astrology?

The search for a pattern. Man is born into a world teeming with life. Everywhere the restless energy of life takes on form, colour, and identity.

Why? For what purpose?

Questions, as old as the human race. The unique characteristic of man, forever asking questions, searching for reasons. Man, just one of the milliard forms of life-expression on Earth and yet he must find a reason for all that is perceived by his conscious mind. Out of the profusion and apparent chaos of life about him he seeks to establish order, to recognise a pattern and purpose embracing all things.

Is there a pattern to life? Or is everything about us simply the chance, chaotic, purposeless outcome of cosmic eruptions? the brainstorm creations within an Idiotic Mind?

Throughout history the profoundest intellectual and philosophical minds have acknowledged that life must have its origins in an Intelligent Mind. Call this Mind or Being what you will. Out of an origin of creative impulse energy has poured forth, devised systems and structures most conveniently adaptable to the environment necessary for growth, self-maintenance and re-creation of the original impulse.

It is not unreasonable to believe that because there *is* a pattern to life as a whole man therefore thinks *in terms of* patterns, and seeks the laws of Nature which will disclose, piece by piece, this whole pattern, and within the whole, the infinite descending scales of patterns within patterns, each in essence the replica of the whole.

Life, with all its complex features and contradictions, is either the unfolding of an intelligently-conceived purpose, to a pre-ordained pattern of growth, or *it is not*. There can be no compromise between what is and what is not.

There are countless ways of seeking evidence of distinct patterns within the world of nature and the growth-functions of man. Astrology is one such path of investigation and interpretation.

Astrology is a system of interpreting *symbols* correlated to human be-haviour and activities.

The symbols which form the basic structure of astrological theory are the Sun, Moon, major planets of the Solar System, and the Earth-sphere as a focal point of reference. These are symbols derived from the cosmic space-time energy-system. In other words, specific geometrical angles and points of mutual contact formed by the planets as they orbit the Sun present continuously changing patterns which, depicted by the symbolical figures in the astrological birth-chart for any given moment of time, correspond to unique patterns of potential behaviour in a man.

The present-day trained astrologer does not think in terms of light-rays or *influences* coming direct from each planet in the way that heat-rays from the Sun on a summer's afternoon stimulate the physical sen-sation of warmth and a feeling of well-being.

The essential correspondence is one of space-time *synchronisation*. The chart of an individual is cast for the *moment* of birth. This moment is considered to be the first intake of breath after severance of the um-bilical cord. In this moment is rooted the whole theory of astrology. At birth the existing pattern of angular relationships between the Sun, planets, and the Earth-angle of the birthplace, synchronise with the total psychological pattern of potentialities. It is the *time* and the *locality* of birth which determine the *individual* nature, distinct from the thousands of other infants born on the same day but at different times and in different localities. Many people do not know their time of birth, but this does not prevent a great deal being known about their general character and temperament from a chart set for noon on the day of birth.

In life nothing stands still: all that is must change. The generation, the flow, the exhaustion of energy is subject to rhythms, cycles of activity and inactivity. Throughout nature one recognises dualities. There is a continuous reconstruction of experience: ebbing and flow-ing, waking and sleeping, growth and decay, birth and death. The dual and complementary aspects create the necessary balance and continuity of life: male and female, positive and negative, night and day, and so on. Through the birth-chart one can discern the rhythmic, cyclic processes in the development of the individual life-pattern, corresponding to the planetary cycles. It must be understood that the chart calculated for a moment of birth describes the *potentialities* of an individual life. It does not represent a 'static quantity'. By further calculations which 'project', as it were, the natal chart 'into the future', the opportunities for un-foldment of these potentialities can be traced; trends in the develop-ment of the life-pattern, likely periods of expansion, frustration, ill-health, misfortune, good favour, and every aspect of the individual's adjustment to the broader collective pattern of life with his fellows. This feature of astrology we call *progressions*.

This is not magic, clairvoyance, make-believe, but interpretation of an individual life-pattern derived from exact astronomical calculations. One of the basic drives in man has surely been the search for *order*; a logical answer to the complexity of life; the assurance that behind the apparent chaos, suffering, and struggle for existence, there is compensa-tion through the working out of a *pattern* – a pattern which ultimately balances all, justifies every effort to do what is right. Some seek this answer in religion, others in science, philosophy, creative art, mystical experiences. Many couldn't care less.

It must be understood that astrology:

1. Does not moralise; the birth-chart indicates weakness or strength in this respect: choice of action is the individual's.

2. Has no religious bias; but indicates the fundamental equality of all men, of all races, each a significant part of the Cosmic Whole we believe to be God.

3. Does not imply a predetermined fate: each man has free-will or choice of action within the necessary limitations of his 'birth-pattern'.

4. Cannot *solve* problems; since, as Dr Carl Jung has said, 'the most important problems of life are all fundamentally insoluble'; they can never be solved, only *outgrown*, and one does this by *accepting* the problem and developing further by means of it. A chart is unique, it can indicate the correct lines of acceptance, and the compensating factors within the nature and life-pattern.

5. Suggests that the correlation between planets and specific growth-formations and activity on Earth is *synchronistic*, in the sense of a coincidence at any moment of time of the *pattern* formed by the interplanetary gravitational fields and causally unrelated energy-systems (e.g., human cells) on Earth. Planets and corresponding energy-systems on Earth are presupposed to have similar mean-ings or values, expressed variably according to the limitations of the form containing the energy-system. In short, planets or their inter-related gravitational fields do not *cause* particular growth-

formations and events on Earth. A certain planetary pattern corresponds with certain growth-formations and energy-system activity because their values in terms of life-promoting or life-sustaining potential are *similar*; and the potential *reaction* of functions related to an energy-system (as the human organs to their cell-components, and to the whole body-system) varies according to the individual concerned.

6. Defines the Sun, Moon, Earth, and planets as *symbols* representing life-principles, inter-related functions within the human being; symbols of unknown cosmic life-qualities.

7. Is, therefore, a system of interpreting planetary motions and their angular relationship to the Earth, in terms of human characteristics, behaviour, and activities.

For the planets to represent symbols for man in his attempt to relate the details of his whole being to an all-embracing Cosmic Pattern is probably crude, clumsy, like a child groping for articulate self-expression with its primitive oral sounds. Yet what of other symbols evolved of necessity by man? The symbols of language, the alphabet. Professor Richard Wilson in *The Miraculous Birth of Language* traces the eventual conversion of oral sound-symbols *of time* into corresponding form-symbols (alphabet, written words) *of space*.

Yet I cannot regard the birth of language or the Solar System as a miracle or accident. Each has its origins in time-space equations. Conscious striving by man to recognise a pattern to his life symbolised elsewhere in the universe of nature *outside himself* is an unconscious motivation of his time-space origins.

Astrology Condemned Through Ignorance. Astrology has stimulated the minds of profound thinkers and scientists for thousands of years, yet it is still condemned as nonsense *by those who have not studied the subject*. Ignorance breeds prejudice, and against the prejudiced there can be no argument. An intelligent discussion, exchange of opinions, with those educated on the subject can promote fresh thought on old ideas, and is a challenge no astrologer would miss. But it is a waste of time to engage in explanation with the critic who has not studied astrology and doesn't intend to enlighten himself with the truth. I must mention the classic remark, already quoted in several astrological books, made by Sir Isaac Newton to the astronomer Halley when the latter scorned his interest in astrology:

'Sir, I have studied it, you have not.'

I cannot think of a better reply to the cynical type of critic.

Fate and free-will. You may think that if the future can be fore-told we have no free-will, we are enmeshed in an irrevocable fate we cannot escape. The astrologer *cannot* predict every event. God forbid that he ever should! He fails (if he foolishly tries to) not only because we still know so little about astrology, but because there is always what Mr. Einstein might call 'the margin of uncertainty'. An astrological aspect with regard to the future can correspond with any one of a variety of possibilities, mostly dependent upon the 'freedom of choice' of the individual concerned, yet the aspect still foretell the actual *trend* of circumstances, or the *nature* of the individual's reaction to the situation.

Religion. The orthodox Christian and Catholic Churches dis-approve of astrology. Usually the argument is (*a*) fate and free-will, (*b*) God never intended man to 'see into the future', (*c*) astrology is blas-phemous, the influence of the Devil, since the Sun and the planets were the pagan gods of primitive man. In truth the astrologer gains a clear insight to religion itself as an essential feature for development in man, being deeply aware of the beautifully created pattern within which our lives are regulated, from which recurring experience a simple yet pro-found philosophy must inevitably be realised.

The Bible is full of astrological references. If astrology is unchristian, a source of evil influence, it is difficult to see why the Three Wise Men played such a significant role at the birth of Jesus. Though astrologers have always known what they were, in *The New English Bible* we read that after the birth of Jesus 'astrologers from the east arrived in Jeru-salem, asking, "Where is the child who is born to be king of the Jews? We have observed the rising of his star . . ." '[1]

Popular astrology. The 'Lucky Star' features in the newspapers and women's periodicals may be the only 'astrology' you have read. These forecasts are based only on the position of the Sun in the 12 Signs of the Zodiac. Each sign covers the identical one-month period of any year (Sun in Aries would be 21st March–20th April). On a cer-tain day all the millions of people born under the same sign will meet 'a tall, handsome stranger' or find it 'a good afternoon for going on a journey'. No wonder that anyone who has not studied the basic con-cepts of astrology thinks of it as an amusing parlour game, a medieval superstition that won't lie down!

Daily forecasts based on the Sun related to the rest of the planets for a given day, and *sensibly* interpreted, can indicate *very general* tendencies

[1] Matthew, ch. 2: v. 2.

in the lives of those born with certain signs strongly emphasised in their *individual* charts (and make-up). For instance, if the planet Saturn were that day very close to the position occupied by the Sun in your chart, there would be a tendency for *limitation* and *frustration* to be felt according to your temperament and circumstances. Character readings based on the Sun-sign alone definitely indicate basic tendencies in the nature, yet only in a general sense when not considered with the whole planetary pattern for a given moment of birth.

Twins. How does an astrologer account for differences in twins born practically together?

The Ascendant, indicative of very *individual* characteristics in the birth-chart, changes its degree every 4 minutes, and the Ascending sign could change within a single minute, introducing marked variations. Twins are sometimes born widely apart, causing appreciable differences. Even Siamese twins *must* differ. There is a 'spiritual factor' in each one of us that cannot be interpreted through astrology. This is the source of free-will; individuality in its truest sense. The birth-chart is essentially the blue-print of the 'Earth vehicle' through which the spirit of man incarnates. Siamese twins will have almost, yet *never* quite, identical bodies, but, as all who believe in a Divine Creator would agree, their own essence of 'eternal spirit'.

Heredity. Through astrology one can get a good indication of what a child will inherit from each parent by comparing their charts with that of the child.

Newly-discovered planets. The discovery of Uranus in 1781, Neptune in 1846, Pluto in 1930, does not mean that all charts set up prior to these discoveries would be wrong since they did not include these bodies. Doctors admit that they still know relatively little about the human body; each year fresh knowledge is added to what is already known, yet the picture is still grossly incomplete. But nobody will ignore the diagnosis of their doctor at this present kindergarten stage of experimentation and research in the adventure of understanding the functioning of the human body and mind. The astrologer, too, is still in the kindergarten stage of experimentation and research in much the same adventure.

Astrology and psychology. The greatest advances in man's understanding of his own nature and the physical properties of his being have rarely been accomplished without almost overwhelming opposition. The pioneer psychologists had their share of ridicule. Today physicists produce nuclear transmutations, and one thinks of those earlier men, the medieval alchemists, who sought for the 'Philospher's Stone', the key formula for transforming base metals into gold. Many truths would never have been bequeathed to us, or remained unrealised until future centuries, had not a minority of the human race through every period of history held firmly to their convictions to establish new truths for the further understanding of man and his place in Nature.

Astrology as practised today by trained astrological-consultants is, by its correlation to modern psychology and the eradication of many muddle-headed esoteric theories and 'fortune-telling sensationalism', far removed from the astrology of even the turn of this century. Yet the basic structure and principles remain much the same. What the early priest-astrologers perceived in the planetary patterns as the influence of their gods, resident in these planets, the astrological-consultant associates with impulses and drives rooted in the unconscious mind of his client, reflected in disposition, emotional response, general behaviour. The stream of thought has spanned the centuries unbroken from its source in antiquity, and with time and distance its course is broader and its banks more fertile with the growth of deeper understanding.

... As the spiritus metallorum *and the astrological components of destiny, the old gods of the planets lasted out many a Christian century. Whereas in the Church the increasing differentiation of ritual and dogma alienated consciousness from its natural roots in the unconscious, alchemy and astrology were ceaselessly engaged in preserving the bridge to nature., i.e., to the unconscious psyche, from decay. Astrology led consciousness back again and again to the knowledge of Heimarmene, that is, the dependence of character and destiny on certain moments in time ...*[1]

Origins. We do not know where or when astrology originated. It would seem to have been a process of observation and accompanying speculation and wonder over a period of centuries before the first man thought to record his observations of the stars – and those 'wandering stars' the planets, and the Moon – and to relate their positions and periodic return to similar points in the heavens with life on Earth.

The earliest traces of astrological knowledge are found among the Chaldeans and the Sumerians, and thence to the Babylonians, Assyrians and Egyptians, suggesting an origin several thousand years before the birth of Christ. To the Chaldeans have been attributed the construction of a learned and profound cosmology, a system of astrotheology. The influence of Chaldean astrology penetrated as far as India, China, Indo-

[1] Dr Carl Jung: *Psychology and Alchemy*, p. 34.

China, and some authorities believe it to have reached even the primitive centres of American civilisation. In the opposite direction this influence spread to Syria, Egypt, and over the whole Roman world. Until the seventeenth century astrology and astronomy were the one science.

We can assume that astrology arose out of the necessity to regulate the growing of crops of the primitive agricultural communities by the seasonal rhythms observed in Nature, as well as through being awe inspired by the patterns of the stars in the night sky. Yet we cannot ignore the possible existence of a substratum of unconscious experience from which sprang the ideas of astrology, religion, architecture, and every significant impulse through which man has created structures for the directing and control of the many desires of his nature. The gods of primitive man, no less than the gods of the varied religions of Twentieth-century man, must have been real to the believer and a source for receiving inner strength. Jung indicates the significance of astrology as an experience derived from the unconscious associations of man with Nature and the Universe: 'As we all know, science began with the stars, and mankind discovered in them the dominants of the unconscious, the "gods", as well as the curious psychological qualities of the zodiac: a complete projected theory of human character. Astrology is a primordial experience similar to alchemy.'[1]

For thousands of years astrology was an accepted feature of man's life. Leaders of great empires planned their strategic moves for the furtherance of power upon the advice of their astrologers. Astrology was no short-lived cult of one nation, or a transient intellectual fashion. Besides those already mentioned, it influenced the cultural development of the Arabians, Greeks, Moors, Hindus, Tibetans, Aztecs, Persians, Israelites, and Europeans. And among the eminent supporters of astrology we find: Confucius, Aristotle, Cicero, Virgil, Dante, Shakespeare, Plato, Yves de Paris, Spinoza, Milton, Bulwer-Lytton, Paracelsus, Leibnitz, Dryden, Schiller, Alexander the Great, Sir Francis Bacon, Henry Van Dyke, Byron, Emerson, Shelley, Napoleon, Caesar, Goethe, Sir Walter Scott, Dr Richard Garnett, John Dee, Nostrodamus, Ptolemy, Baron Napier of Merchiston (inventor of logarithms), Pythagoras, and the 'Father of Medicine' Hippocrates.

Above all, five of the greatest scientists and astronomers were also astrologers: Johannes Kepler, Sir Isaac Newton, Tycho Brahe, Nicolaus Copernicus, and Galileo Galilei. Their immortal contributions to

[1] Jung: *Psychology and Alchemy*, p. 234.

science are rightly acclaimed as the achievements of genius, yet blind distinction is made to any reference to their interest in astrology by either ignoring it or passing it off as rather unfortunate and due to the superstitious age they lived in! Yet these were men who risked torture or death at the stake by defying traditional scientific and philosophical theories. Astrology in their time was universally accepted, yet even so, if either of these had tested it and found it to be nonsense they would hardly have continued practising the art or writing books relating to new astrological theories.

Kepler's three great laws of planetary motion, which confirmed the Copernicus heliocentric theory that the Sun and not the Earth was the centre of the universe, establishing a new era for astronomy, and were one of the pillars on which Newton based his theory of gravitation, were the outcome of painstaking work in which astrology was the very mainspring.

In his great work *Harmonices mundi* Kepler stressed his theories on the 'harmony of the spheres', and his belief that 'the soul bears within itself the idea of the zodiac, or rather of its centre. . . .'[1]

John Flamsteed, the first Astronomer-Royal of England, chose the time (3.14 p.m., 10th August 1675) and calculated the chart for the founding of the famous Greenwich Observatory – an excellent example of an election chart (chart calculated to a chosen 'favourable' time, usually for starting a new venture).

And today? In the past thirty years there has been a tremendous surge of renewed interest in astrology. Increasing numbers of scientists, psychologists, teachers and welfare workers are being trained to the serious application of the subject by the Mayo School of Astrology. I cannot speak for other schools and evening classes. Outstandingly successful astrological/psychological research is being undertaken by Dr Michael Gauquelin in France, and by Professor Hans Eysenck and myself in the U.K., and many other serious workers.

Astrology is a subject that cannot be lightly dismissed. Nobody, today, with an astrological book stuck in their pocket need fear ridicule. As we turn the pages of this book let us remember the words of Sir William Crooks:

To stop short in any research that bids fair to widen the gates of knowledge, to recoil from fear of difficulty or adverse criticism, is to bring reproach upon science.

[1] *The Interpretation of Nature and the Psyche*, by Jung & Pauli, p. 182.

Circles within circles

If you look at the diagram (Figure 1) of an astrological birth-chart, you will notice that everything is contained within a circle. At the centre of this circle is a smaller circle. The symbols refer to the planets and signs, but don't bother about these yet. I just want to convey to you this idea of 'the circle within a circle'. The inner circle represents the Earth. The outer circle represents the apparent path in the celestial sphere which the Sun and the planets seem to describe about the Earth. We know that in reality the Sun is the centre of the Solar System, that the planets trace an elliptical and not a circular path about the Sun.

Astrology, however, is a system of symbols. These outer and inner circles which are part of the basic framework of the birth-chart symbolise the Earth-sphere as the centre of the celestial sphere. This is perfectly correct from our angle of looking out at the rest of the universe. Now let us enlarge upon this idea of 'the circle within a circle' as we briefly view our own planet in its true perspective in the universe.

Stellar systems or galaxies. The observable universe contains perhaps ten thousand million galaxies. Galaxies are complex organisations of stars, gas, dust. They vary considerably in size and structure. An average galaxy may have a population of a thousand million stars. We may appreciate how difficult it is for the human mind to comprehend such a congregation of star systems, when we realise that our own Sun is our nearest *star* – which is an average distance of 93 million miles from the Earth! What may appear in the night sky to our naked eye as a bright hazy blur or star could be a complete galaxy of a thousand million stars, billions of miles beyond our own galactic system!

The galaxy. *The* galaxy is the galactic system our own Earth planet belongs to. It is sometimes called the 'Milky Way system', because this luminous belt composed of millions of stars and clouds of interstellar dust that can be seen on a clear night appears to be the encircling edges of our 'flattened' or lense-shaped stellar system.

Our galaxy is one of the largest known, containing perhaps 100 thousand million stars.

Our own Sun is the centre of the Solar System (Figure 3). But the Sun is also revolving round a centre, the *galactic centre*, round which the millions of other stars in *the* galaxy revolve. The Sun is travelling at a speed of over 12 miles per second, in the approximate direction of Right Ascension 277°, its position relative to the Earth about the end of December annually. Therefore, each year in December the Earth is directly behind the Sun according to the direction in which the Sun is moving forward round the centre of the galaxy. At the end of June the Earth is virtually ahead of the Sun, at a point where the Sun will be three months later! The Sun completes one circuit of the galaxy in about 200 million years.

Astrology is only concerned with our own Solar System for interpreting a birth-chart. Yet we should be aware of the cosmic laws governing the universe, from which arise circles within circles, cycles within cycles. An ancient Hermetic axiom states, 'as above, so below'. The macrocosm (great world) is repeated in the microcosm (little world). The human body is composed of billions of cells, each cell 'is a life centred in itself, managing itself, feeding and breathing for itself, separately born and destined separately to die. Further, it is a life helped by, and in its turn helping, the whole assembly, which latter is the corporate individual.'[1]

Each cell has its central nucleus, the most vital structure in its organised mass; extract this and the cell dies. The heart of man corresponds to the nucleus of the cell: extract this and man dies. The Sun is the heart or nucleus of the Solar System: obliterate the Sun and the planetary system would disintegrate. The galactic centre is the nucleus for our galaxy. And so with all stars and galaxies of stars. Life is one great energy-system. Within this energy-system are infinite aggregations of lesser energy-systems. Each is concerned with maintaining itself, yet is dependent upon its environment and other energy-systems, each giving and taking, creating and maintaining the vital equilibrium. Whether the energy-system is galaxy, star, planet, man, atom, all is pervaded by radiation.

[1] Sir Charles Sherrington: *Man on his Nature.*

With this picture of *interdependence*, from galaxy to atom, the astrological theory of correspondences should be realised as perfectly logical reasoning, warranting fullest scientific investigation.

The solar system. This consists of the Sun and nine major planets; several thousand minor planets or asteroids; satellites of planets, as the Earth's Moon; comets, meteors, interplanetary dust.

For convenience astrologers refer to the Sun as a planet. It is a star, being self-luminous. In this way it resembles the countless other so-called *fixed* stars, termed such because they always appear to remain in the same position in the sky. This is due to their immense distances from the Earth. Actually all stars are in motion and subject to the gravitational control of the stellar system they belong to. Stars are completely gaseous, unlike planets which are solid matter.

The constellations. Constellations are groups of stars. Those having identical names to the Zodiacal Signs have only a mythological association with these Signs.

The planets: life-principles

The 3 basic factors for interpreting the growth-pattern symbolised in a birth-chart are:

The *planets*, as the Sun's satellites;

The *Signs of the Zodiac*, correlative to the Earth-Sun angular relationship (equator-ecliptic);

The *mundane houses*, determined by the intersection of ecliptic-horizon.

The *planets* symbolise basic human functions, life-principles. Apart from the Sun and Moon, discounting the Earth, there are eight planets to consider. The Earth is represented by the 12 *mundane houses*, the spheres of human activity. These functions (planets) are regulated and integrated by the Sun. The magnetic field of the Earth-Sun angular relationship corresponds to the 12 *signs*, which provide varied attitudes of expression for the functions represented by the planets.

First, you will learn about the planets. In Figure 2 these are shown placed against the signs associated with them (traditionally a planet is said to be *ruler* of one or more signs). In Figure 3 you can see the planets in their orbits round the Sun, though of necessity the diagram is grossly out of proportion. The planets revolve from east to west *relative to the Sun*, but as seen from the Earth they appear to move from west to east *relative to the background of stars*. The arrows from the Earth (⊕) in the direction of the planets are to convey to you the idea of the Earth as the central point of reference. In this sense the Earth might be viewed as the centre of the astrological chart, and if all the planets were placed at the same distance from the Earth the diagram would show how they would appear in the birth-chart.

Focal points of energy. The planets represent *focal points of unconscious energies*, associated with basic life-principles. Life as a whole is

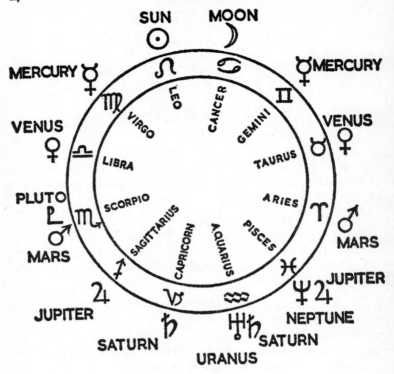

FIGURE 2

The Planets and their associated Signs

The Sun enters:

Aries around March 21	Libra around September 23
Taurus around April 20	Scorpio around October 23
Gemini around May 21	Sagittarius around November 22
Cancer around June 21	Capricorn around December 22
Leo around July 23	Aquarius around January 20
Virgo around August 23	Pisces around February 19

an energy-system. The Sun is an energy-system, within the energy-system of the galaxy. Man is an energy-system, featured by the structure and substances of his body, and regulated, activated, and capable of conscious discrimination, dependent upon the functioning of the life-principles within him by which his being is related to the infinite cosmic energy-systems.

I must stress the idea of man and planets as energy-systems function-

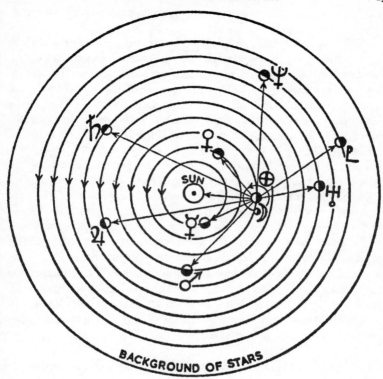

FIGURE 3
The Scheme of the Solar System

ing according to patterns of time-space origin. You will more clearly understand astrological symbology if you learn to think of the human cell, man, and planet correlated to time-space patterns which determine the characteristics of growth, and in man, the transmutation of unconscious impulses into conscious perception and thinking. Matter would be formless and without purpose were it not shaped and energised by specific geometrical time-space patterns. The 'miracle' which transforms a single fertilised human cell stage by stage into an individual creature, with liver, heart, fingers, stomach, nerve-fibres systematically arranged in *preparedness* for specific functions, unfolds to a distinct time-space pattern. It is as if the millions of microscopic cells participating in the adventure could anticipate the demands and challenge of life ultimately to be brought into existence by the *mathematics of time and space*.

Archetypal impulses. It is hard to believe the personification of the planets and choice of names could be pure chance. As already quoted, Jung has said that 'astrology represents the summation of all the psychological knowledge of antiquity'. The essence of all truth is first given to man in symbols from his own unconscious, which is rooted in the Collective Unconscious linking the minds of all humanity to an eternal pulse of life. In thinking of the planets as symbolising focal points of unconscious energies these may also be understood as *archetypal impulses*. The same archetypal impulses felt and personified by our ancestors as gods in Nature corresponding to fundamental desires in man. By archetypal impulses I mean original forces of Nature necessary for regulating man's growth and evolution, which stimulated his deepest instinctive responses before even he crawled from the primeval swamps, and which as an unbroken stream of energy throughout thousands of years still dominate our waking and sleeping phases of life through the unconscious. Probably the less consciously-awakened that man is, the more real and factual are these archetypal forces registered through his psychic faculties, and it is not difficult to realise why these experiences became projected into the conscious mind as gods – planetary gods even – personifying his deepest feelings.

Keywords formula for interpreting planetary life-principles

Sun: Principle of *self-integration*.

Moon: Principle of *rhythms* through instinctive response, assimilation, reflection.

Mercury: *Communicative* principle through mental and nervous co-ordination, transmission.

Venus: *Uniting* principle through sympathy, evaluation, feeling.

Mars: Principle of *activity* through enterprise, self-assertion, energetic expression.

Jupiter: Principle of *expansion* through growth, materially and by understanding.

Saturn: *Formative* principle through restriction, discipline, rigidity.

Uranus: Principle of *deviation* through invention, independence, drastic change.

Neptune: *Refining* principle through dissolution, subtlety, immateriality, sensitivity.

Pluto: *Transforming* principle through elimination, renewal.

These keywords will convey to you the basic function and principle of each planet, and help you to memorise these more quickly. These are my choice of keywords, though in principle similar to those chosen by other astrologers. Later you may prefer to make a slight variation to the above. Acknowledgment must be made to Margaret Hone[1] who devised her own method of combining the keywords of planets, signs and houses, which greatly simplifies interpretation. A similar method will be employed when we come to interpretation.

An entire book could be written on the planets alone, and their apparent astronomical correlation with cycles of mankind's evolutionary development. The definitions which follow aim to describe the essential nature of the functions within man symbolised by the planets. Special emphasis is given to physiological relationships. As you read the definition for each planet, bear in mind their keywords.

SUN

Life-principle: power of self-integration, wholeness of being.

Symbol: ⊙ Circle with a dot in its centre. The dot signifies the nuclei, seed of potential individual manifestation of human spirit or consciousness within the Collective Unconscious sphere. The circle, in one sense, implies completeness, divine spirit.

In *mythology* the Sun was personified as the all-pervading creative power in Nature, the masculine principle of Fatherhood (God) and authority. Sun-worship of primitive peoples was undoubtedly natural awe and respect for this source of energy, light, heat and growth contrasting with the feared death-like cold and darkness of the night.

Astronomically the Sun is the central governing force for its own system of planets.

Physiologically the functions of the heart, circulatory system, and thymus are associated with the Sun. Afflictions to the Sun suggest a tendency to disorders or disease through these parts, other factors considered.

The function of the *heart* clearly corresponds to the Sun's cosmic role as the vital, energising factor in life. In the *circulatory system* we see how this purposeful, controlling influence is transmitted and integrates every part of the body to the organism as a whole, with its intricate network of arteries and veins by which warmth, vital energy, nutrients, waste material are accordingly distributed. The essential function of the heart, however, appears not to be as a *causal* process of life but, as Dr Rudolph

[1] *The Modern Textbook of Astrology.*

Steiner has indicated, an *effect*. The heart is not the cause, or origin, of an individual, any more than its pumping of blood through the arteries is the sustainer of life. True, the heart stops beating and the man dies. But the heart will not stop beating of its own accord. The heart's motion expresses the *equilibrium* it maintains between opposing forces working through the body, and is the result, the evidence, of interacting formative as well as dispersive processes. Life does not enter through the heart alone, but through each vital organ. But the heart governs and regulates the equilibrium of the whole body, which determines its unique character, records the prevailing tone of health or sickness. The most evident activity of the *thymus*, one of the endocrine glands, corresponds with the formative years of childhood, suggesting a significant role in *regulating the rhythms of growth* and delaying puberty until the required formation has been achieved. A recent theory is that the thymus may also be responsible for the *immunological activity* of the body against foreign antigens[1] (bacteria, etc.), and therefore may be 'intimately involved in the development of those reactions which make each one of us a *biologically unique individual*'.[2]

Psychologically, by sign position, the Sun signifies one's attitude to the Collective Unconscious streams underlying human nature, in terms of the respective group-characteristics associated with the sign. It does *not* represent individuality, but a typical process whereby one can most naturally *integrate* each feature of the Psyche into a unique individual represented by the *whole* chart-pattern.

The Sun is specially associated with the sign Leo, and the 5th house.[3]

MOON

Life-principle: Rhythms, through instinctive response, assimilation, reflection.

Symbol: ☽ The incomplete circle: the mind, evolving human spirit. Or the dual nature of human spirit, part conscious, part unconscious.

In *mythology* the Moon was personified by the Greeks as a goddess, *Luna*. The waxing of the Moon was likened to 'the swelling of a pregnant woman's womb, the "conjunction" (*suzugía*) of the sun and the new moon to the copulation of man and woman (Greek: *súnodos*, Latin *coitus*), whence the term 'synodic month' for the period between

[1] Sir MacFarlane Burnet, O.M., F.R.S., in the *New Scientist*, 27th September 1962.

[2] Editorial, *The British Medical Journal*, 29th September 1962.

[3] See Chapter 8 for a description of the houses.

two "new moons".'[1] The ancients associated fertility, growth and decay, with the lunation phases, which has been variously confirmed by science. For instance, the Moon influences plant growth, fluids of the Earth, and the Swedish scientist Svante Arrhenius statistically verified that the sidereal lunar month corresponds with the female menstruation cycle.

Astronomically the Moon is the Earth's satellite, but it does not revolve round the Earth in the manner of a satellite to its centre of attraction. The Earth's pull upon the Moon is but secondary to that of the Sun, which is the common centre of gravity for both bodies. The Earth-Moon system is, in effect, a double planet. Symbolically this suggests the *dual nature* of the Moon, divided between the pull of the Sun (spirit) and the Earth (physical body). Its rhythmically wavering cycles of *response* to the attractions of the Earth-Sun polarity are reflected in the largely lunar cause of the *ebb and flow* of the tides.

Physiologically the functions of the digestive system, lymphatic system, synovial fluids, stomach, breasts, ovaries, pancreas, and the sympathetic nervous system are associated with the Moon. Afflictions to the Moon suggest a tendency to disorders or disease through these parts, other factors considered.

The function of the Moon corresponds to the *organic medium of fluids and lymph* which filter through the body, nourishing, helping the process of digestion, protecting vital organs with 'cushions of fluid', lubricating, and periodically preparing the moist, maternal receptacle for impregnation. The *pancreas* regulates sugar supplies for energy; low blood-sugar produces 'emotional instability', a recognised symptom of an afflicted Moon. The Moon is associated with the automatic and spontaneous reflexes of the *sympathetic nervous system*, which besides being connected with nutrition, elimination, and protection of the organism, is intimately associated with emotions, affections, desires. The 'influence' of the Full Moon upon the emotionally disturbed or lunatics (*lunar*: Moon) is well-known.

The Moon factor is the mediator between past and present, accumulating the whole story of man's personal evolution within the fluids of brain and body; each new experience registered, unconsciously digested, and transmuted into the instinctive functions. Thus, *psychologically* are erected protective forms of *habit-patterns*, instinctive behaviour and response. It has been traditionally thought that people with the Moon emphasised in their chart (and personal make-up) tend to cling to the

[1] Robert Eisler: *The Royal Art of Astrology*, p. 138.

past. If they do, it is because of the interaction of other factors. It is not the Moon alone holds them to the past. The Moon establishes an essential rhythm in the body and instinctive mind. An ebb and flow of sensation and emotional experience. An ebb and flow that maintains the periodical need for man to withdraw into past experience, memory, or to draw on the past, for the revitalising of mind and body, as these are revitalised with sleep. It is this link with the past, contained within man, that has been misunderstood. Restlessness and changeableness are often traced to the Moon.

The Moon is connected with the *deepest* associations with one's family and ancestors, especially the mother, often extended to national patriotism. Possibly this springs from the powerful mother-child relationship begun in the womb, nurtured through the breast secretions, both functions primarily related to the Moon. Hence, the Moon indicates the 'mother-complex'.

The Moon is specially associated with the sign Cancer, and the 4th house.

MERCURY

Life-principle: Communication, through mental and nervous co-ordination and transmission.

Symbol: ☿ Contains the 3 basic symbols: the half-circle (human spirit or mind) poised over the circle (divine spirit) and the cross (matter). Derived from the 'staff of Mercurius', the caduceus, consisting of two serpents around a rod, indicating the riddle of life. To understand this riddle requires mind and reason.

In *mythology* Mercury was personified by the Romans as Mercurius, the divine winged Grecian god Hermes, the swift-footed messenger of the gods. Regarded as the god of eloquence, cunning, invention, roads, commerce.

Astronomically Mercury is nearest the Sun, from which it can never be more than 28° (as viewed from the Earth). Is unique among the planets, being smallest in size and mass, has the greatest linear speed, shortest sidereal period or year. Only Pluto's orbit is more eccentric. Is at the same time the hottest and the coldest planet, as (like the Moon to the Earth) it always turns the same face to the Sun, one side being in perpetual sunlight, the other in perpetual shadow. Symbolically, perhaps, since Mercury represents mentality, this dual aspect denotes the constant and necessary distinction between the conscious and unconscious in man.

Physiologically Mercury is associated with the central nervous system, the brain generally, respiratory system, thyroid, all sense perception and sensory organs. Afflictions to Mercury suggest a tendency to disorders or disease through these parts, other factors considered.

Typical of the Mercurian process is the basic behavioural pattern characteristic of all *nervous* organisations: excitation, conduction, integration. Integration by reason and logic through the medium of *brain* and *central nervous system*, which serves conscious functions, transforms sensations into perceptions, is the coordinator of all nerve impulses and reflexes. Here is the seat of the will, the apparatus for thinking. Yet not only through the brain but with the whole organism man thinks, and this is the principle of Mercury, the interpreter of the unconscious, the transmitter, messenger, communicator. Through the *nervous and sensory systems* and the *lungs* man receives the impress of his environment, the brain analyses, and he learns to relate and communicate to the exterior world his own unique nature. Through the lungs oxygen is adapted for conveyance to all parts of the body. Associated with the *thyroid* is the control of combustion of air in breathing; regulation of the *rate* of metabolism and energy production; expression of movement, volatility; nervous reactions; critical functional *changes* during life; regulation of growth and mental development.

Psychologically the urge to know, to be conscious, to communicate knowledge to others. Venus is the desire to communicate one's total conception of oneself as a process of the *feelings*, to *relate* oneself, to others. The Mercurian urge is to communicate knowledge, facts, and to teach, in terms of the *mental* processes and intellect. Mercury is unemotional. Thus Mercury shows the ability to consciously interpret all that is continually passing through the brain, whether from the unconscious, the 'memory cells', the impact of exterior life on the senses, intuitive impressions, nerve reflexes, and so on. The mind is normally accepted to be the individual spirit which expresses itself and controls its physical counterpart through the instrument of the brain. Mercury represents this instrument or apparatus in all its ramifications of cerebro-spinal system and nerve structures. Jung calls the mind the Psyche,[1] embracing both the conscious and the unconscious aspects of man which function together as a process, dynamic and self-regulating. Mercury, therefore, represents only one feature of the mind.

Changes, readjustments are necessary, indeed, inevitable: life is complex streams of energy in a ceaseless flux of form creation and recon-

[1] See *An Introduction to Jung's Psychology*, by Frieda Fordham (Pelican Books).

struction, and the Mercury principle in man registers these changes, and is, it would seem, the plastic formative force which determines the nature of *necessary changes in the individual.*

Traditionally Mercury is said to have no nature of its own, and reflects what it receives from aspecting planets. This is nonsense. Mercury represents a function, a life-principle, and cannot be other than itself, any more than the kidney can adopt the nature of the heart or the heart that of the kidney. All planets can be said to reflect the light of the Sun, which as a star creates its own light, but the essential quality, the unique function, derives from the planet, and can only *interact* with the principle of another planet, never take on the other's nature.

Mercury is specially associated with the signs Gemini and Virgo, and the 3rd and 6th houses.

VENUS

Life-principle: Unity, through sympathy, evaluation, feeling.
Symbol: ♀ Represents the circle (divine spirit) above the cross (matter). In biology and medicine it is still the symbol for the feminine principle.

In *mythology* Venus was originally a Latin goddess of the spring; later identified with the Greek Aphrodite, goddess of love and beauty, derived from *fero*, to bear, bring forth, produce.

Astronomically is the brightest object in the sky after the Sun and Moon, and comes closer to the Earth than any other body except the Moon and some comets and asteroids. Is never more than 48° from the Sun (viewed from the Earth).

Physiologically is associated with the lumbar region, venous circulation, parathyroids, and indirectly (through affinity with Taurus and Libra) the throat and kidneys. Afflictions to Venus suggest disorders or disease through these parts, other factors considered.

Symbolically the *venous veins* gather the blood from every area of the body and conduct it back to the heart, a *centripetal* process. People in whom the Venus characteristics are emphasised often experience gastric, *kidney* or *circulatory* troubles because of an excessive fondness for rich foods; also *throat* and *genital* afflictions (Taurus-Scorpio polarity) due to an easily stimulated erotic and amorous nature. The *parathyroids* regulate the metabolism of calcium and phosphorus. These are indispensable for the building of the skeleton framework which gives *form* and *holds together* the human organism, corresponding to the Venus principle of the welding together of complementary factors, the need for a harmonious pattern as a basis to form. Phosphorus derives from the Greek and Latin, light-bearer, morning star. The para-thyroids are complementary to the thyroid (of Mercury, producing movement, volatility, nervous activity). Thus, with the parathyroids under-developed or functioning inadequately there is an increase in thyroid secretion, the individual becomes pathologically nervous, irritable, oversensitive. Working normally, the Venus nature is evident in the warmth of feeling, passivity, steadiness, serenity. There is a lack of a *wholesome attitude toward life* when calcium and phosphorus are deficient in the blood.[1]

Psychologically the function for judging and valuing experience through the *feelings*, as opposed to rationalised judgment and evaluation. It is always a centripetal process, an essentially inner and subjective experience. Venus represents the feminine impulse in *both* sexes, as Mars represents the masculine. Venus has to receive, Mars gives. Venus is soft and passive, Mars hard and assertive. Venus is unity of purpose, cooperation, Mars is singleness of purpose. Venus symbolises the function in Nature that balances, harmonises, resolves, unifies, smooths out the rough and the discordant. The impulse is *pure feeling*. It is that which must relate factors. It is the need to appreciate and to be appreciated. It is the power behind loving, need for affection, desire for the beautiful, the artistic, aesthetic, for that which is priceless. It is the feeling within the creative impulse: the essence of creativity. It is not the physical aspect of sex: it is the desire to unite opposites, to re-create the image of oneself in one's opposite, and of the opposite in oneself. Venus, through the function which evaluates and desires for itself, is also associated with the ability to acquire money and accumulate possessions, or how one may attract good fortune.

Venus is specially associated with the signs Taurus and Libra, and the 2nd and 7th houses.

MARS

Life-principle: Activity, through enterprise, self-assertion, energetic expression.

Symbol: ♂ The cross (matter) over the circle (divine spirit), implying a function essentially physical and sensual in expression. The arrow suggests the initiatory and objective attitude. Used in medicine and biology for the masculine principle.

In *mythology* Mars was personified by the Romans as a war-god. Originally he was their nature-god protecting crops and herds, ward-

[1] Prof. V. H. Mottram: *The Physical Basis of Personality*, p. 76.

ing off pests, storms and droughts. Identified with the Greek war-god Ares. Hindu equivalent was Indra, slayer of serpents and dragons. The Babylonians called it the Star of Death, associated with carnage, plagues, disaster.

Astronomically is sometimes called the 'red planet' due to the red light it reflects – an interesting 'coincidence' when one thinks of the blood, war and inflammatory connections!

Physiologically associated with the muscular system, urogenital system and gonads (sex glands), adrenals, sympathetic nervous system, red corpuscles of the blood, kidneys. Afflictions to Mars suggest a tendency to disorders or disease through these parts, other factors considered. People whose charts show Mars strongly emphasised are prone to inflammations, fevers, cuts, burns, scalds.

Mars represents the general factor in the physical body of attack and resistance against disease and foreign bodies, and the elimination of waste products. Inflammations and fevers are an example. Mars function is centrifugal, energy flowing outwards to the periphery, to every orifice and each pore of the skin. We see the connection with the *urogenital system*: the *bladder* containing waste fluids, eliminating these as urine, the *male testes* from which sperm is discharged, the shedding of eggs from the *female ovaries*. Overheating of the body, and the pores release sweat. The *male sexual organ* is significantly resembled in erection in the Mars glyph, expressive of the phallus image that was once widely worshipped as a symbol of the generative power in nature. Essentially Mars indicates the *physical* aspect of sex, and the corresponding desire, passion or lust that seeks sensual gratification. Venus represents the creative impulse, the initial attraction between the sexes, the awakening need to reproduce or to consummate the love-union. Mars supplies the necessary apparatus and *sensual* stimulus. *Iron*, which supplies warmth, has always been associated with Mars. The *muscular system* is the intricate machinery by which activity and manipulation of the whole skeleton and functional processes within the organism can be performed, and through which *power* is expressed.

The *adrenals* have been called the 'fight and flight' glands of the endocrine system, because under the stress of fear or anger its secretions pour into the bloodstream 'stimulating the activity of the heart, raising the blood-pressure, deepening the respiration, increasing the blood-sugar that has to supply the fuel for the muscles, and generally preparing the animal for flight, or fight, upon which its life may depend'.[1] Auto-

[1] Kenneth Walker: *Diagnosis of Man*, pp. 37–8.

matic response and emergency preparation is then the function of the *sympathetic nervous system* which is regulated most particularly by adrenaline. The adrenals play a vital part in energy exchanges of the body, control sex activities, promote a system of resistance to disease or for self-preservation. Louis Berman has called the adrenal-controlled man or woman the 'Atlas of the twentieth-century world'. Over-activity, or a tumour, of these glands promotes masculine character-istics in a woman. The Mars principle can be recognised working through the sympathetic nervous system in its protection of the organ-ism, helping with elimination, and as an intimate link with the source of emotions and desires situated at the back of the brain. Traditionally the *kidneys* are associated with Libra and Venus, but hormone secre-tions from the adrenals control the kidneys' function, which is prob-ably why I have often found an afflicted Mars as a likely indicator of kidney complaints.

Psychologically the impulse to be active, energetic, self-assertive. It is emotional energy, sensuality, desire to fight, pioneer, take the initiative. It is the sexual urge, energy and potency. In itself it is neither construc-tive nor destructive. The mode or purpose of applied energy depends upon the directive as determined by the interaction of Mars with other factors in the chart. It may convey the seeds for new beginnings but it only becomes a fertile and creative process when other factors can be constructively combined with it. It is the masculine principle that is non-creative without its feminine counterpart. An afflicted Mars im-plies a tendency to be cruel, impatient, destructive, recklessly impul-sive, aggressive.

Mars is specially associated with the signs Aries and Scorpio, and the 1st and 8th houses.

JUPITER

Life-principle: Expansion, through growth, materially and by understanding.

Symbol: ♃ The half circle (mind, human spirit) above the horizon or level of the cross (matter). Denotes the aspect of human spirit that must expand and develop a higher consciousness beyond, yet out of, physical experience.

In *mythology* Jupiter was personified as the Roman deity of the same name, the most powerful and the highest among the gods, the seer, guardian of law, protector of justice and virtue. Identified with the mighty Zeus of the Greeks and the Scandinavian Thor.

Astronomically is the largest planet. In both volume and mass it is greater than all the planets put together, though its density is less than one-quarter of the Earth's.

Physiologically is associated with the liver, the disposition of fats, posterior lobe of the pituitary gland. Afflictions to Jupiter suggest a tendency to disorders or disease through these parts, other factors considered.

Jupiter represents in the physical body expansion, protection, healing, and the prime factor of growth. The *liver* is the largest gland in the human body. Jupiter is essentially associated with the liver's function of purifying the blood, production of glycogen, destruction of poisons and microbes; Saturn, secretion of bile. Formation of *fats* provides protective layers for various bodily purposes. Through this function Jupiter is associated with the 'fair, fat, and forty' middle-age spread. The typical joviality of outsized individuals is attributed to an active Jupiter function; fatty degeneration of muscles, enlarged organs, tumours, to Jupiter afflicted. The *pituitary gland* (combining posterior and anterior lobes) is recognised by endocrinologists as the central regulator of all hormone production, except perhaps that of the pineal. If removed from a young animal growth ceases; if underdeveloped in a human, growth is stunted, overactive the result may be gigantism (a giant). Growth is the mutual role of Jupiter-Saturn. The *posterior lobe of the pituitary* is a healing and harmonising function.

Psychologically the urge to expand the consciousness, to understand (distinct from mere accumulation of knowledge), to mature. It is the regulator of uniform growth throughout the organism. It is that within us which seeks to develop certain features to *compensate* for inadequacies or failures elsewhere. It is *conscience* in the fullest sense. Hence, association of this principle in man with the qualities of justice with mercy; an inner sense of law, order, morals, religious convictions; a desire to protect, heal, preserve; ability to bring 'growth processes' to maturity, fulfilment, and to gain good fortune and favour. If Mars is the energy for growth, Jupiter is the means and the capacity. An afflicted Jupiter implies a tendency to exaggerate, to be extravagant, lawless, conceited, procrastinating.

Jupiter is specially associated with the signs Sagittarius and Pisces, and the 9th and 12th houses.

SATURN

Life-principle: Formative, through restriction, discipline, rigidity.
Symbol: ♄ The cross (matter) taking precedence over the half-circle

(mind, human spirit). Symbolic of the limitation and density of the physical, through which the human spirit, evolving as mind, must penetrate to make further growth and consciousness. It has been identified with the scythe of the god Cronus, or Time (Father time).

In *mythology* Saturn was personified by the Romans as Saturnus, god of agriculture, founder of civilisation and social order. Identified with Cronus (Kronos) the Greek god of Time and mundane time-cycles, who was originally a harvest god. The planet was called 'Seb, god of earth' by the Egyptians; Seb also meaning 'Time'. In myths and legend Saturn is depicted as the reaper, the time-keeper with hour-glass and scythe, the symbol of the limit of life's span that must inevitably end with death.

Astronomically the unique feature is Saturn's system of rings which encircle the planet's equator. Astrologically this ring system can symbolise the 'ring-pass-not' of occult teachings; the cosmic thought or tone energised through the planet, crystallised in graphic representation of its principle of limits and boundaries.

Physiologically associated with the skeletal system, skin, teeth, anterior lobe of the pituitary gland, gall bladder, spleen, pneumogastric or vagus nerve. Afflictions to Saturn suggest a tendency to disorders or disease through these parts, other factors considered.

Saturn represents in the physical body form and structure, crystallisation, constriction, and the time-factor of growth. The *skeleton* gives exterior and interior form, support, and poise. Another vital factor connects the bone structure with Saturn: the time-factor of growth. From an anatomical viewpoint the most reliable way of assessing the *age* of an individual is by examination of the skeleton and the teeth.[1] Crystallisations, acid-formation in the joints, congestion or retention of fluids, blockages, hardening of arteries, atrophy, malnutrition, slowing down and cooling of the whole system, are typical Saturn afflictions. Also, chronic, deep-seated ailments.

We may think of Saturn representing a necessary force for keeping life and energy within specific bounds, regulating and controlling growth by restrictive processes of purely 'time-origin'. The principle of Saturn corresponding to the function of the *skin* periphery is not the protective aspect, but a necessary boundary, structural limit, formative material. The *anterior lobe of the pituitary* has been called the 'conductor of the endocrine orchestra', such an important role does it play. Its secretions promote masculine traits, are essential for growth, especi-

[1] R. J. Harrison: *Man the Peculiar Animal*, p. 282.

ally the structure of bones and muscles, and regulates the sex glands. An afflicted Saturn is the chief cause of gallstones. The Saturn processes cause a natural lowering of temperature, and tendency to dryness, bareness, barrenness, gauntness.

Psychologically the urge for developing self-discipline, self-consciousness. Originating as an unconscious process it is the time-keeper within the body and Psyche, regulating a distinct time-system, the tempo of which is set by the condition of the heart. Without the function corresponding to Saturn man would not think clearly, logically, or be able to concentrate, or formulate concrete, constructive ideas and plans. It represents the builder in man, the architect, contemplative monk, the power for sustained, monotonous, laborious work requiring patience and sense of duty. It is the serious and reflective attitude in man; the need for realistic, practical, resourceful and responsible handling of life's affairs. Essentially this is man's awareness to reality, his central process of constructing an Ego Complex, i.e., the knowing, self-conscious aspect of his Psyche that realises itself as a separate being, or through which one might experience an acute aloneness or isolation from one's fellows. In the chart Saturn represents the mainspring for fear, suffering, self-denial, sense of personal inadequacy. It can provide the key to inhibitions and personal 'defence mechanisms', or the reasons for a 'psychological act of withdrawal' from certain experiences. An afflicted Saturn implies a tendency to selfishness, heartlessness, cruelty, depressive moods, perhaps a life of much hardship, sorrow, ill-health.

Saturn is specially associated with the signs Capricorn and Aquarius, and the 10th and 11th houses.

THE EXTRA-SATURNIAN PLANETS

These are the three planets beyond the orbit of Saturn: Uranus, Neptune, Pluto. Their functions suggest the formation of *impersonal* characteristics in the individual, whereas the planets inside the orbit of Saturn (including Saturn) correspond to *personal* characteristics.

This theory is based on the average time taken by each planet to pass through the signs. The Moon is the fastest, going through all 12 signs in less than a month. It represents a very personal factor, since the total births in any one month can be divided into 12 types so far as just the Moon is concerned. Pluto is the planet furthest from the Sun, taking about 248 years to pass through the whole cycle of the Zodiac, an average of 20 years in each sign. Thus, Pluto represents an impersonal factor, since all born during an average 20-years period when Pluto is in the same sign would have similar 'Pluto characteristics'. Likewise, Uranus (7 years in a sign) and Neptune (14 years in a sign) provide gradual changes and developments in the *general* characteristics of whole groups or generations of humanity. Naturally there are as many subtle variations in the strength of these characteristics as there are individuals born in each period, and these characteristics become more personal and conscious factors whenever either of these three planets are strongly placed in an individual chart.

The 7 personal planets were those the ancients could see with the naked eye. The '7' is symbolised in myth and in the scriptures as principles of the One, a mystic number, a symbol of perfection. The Seven Spirits before the Throne of God, seven Archangels, seven lamps, seven eyes 'which are the seven spirits of God' (Rev. 5: 6), the seven stars 'are the angels of the seven churches' (Rev. 1: 20). 'Wisdom hath builded her own house, she hath hewn out her seven pillars' (Prov. 9: 1). Likewise the seven planets, their seven principles, may be realised as seven pillars upon which the house (physical body) of man is built within which to contain his spirit. The seven days of the week, seven primary colours and notes of music, have their correlation with these planets.

URANUS

Life-principle: Deviation, through invention, independence, drastic change.

Symbol: ♅ Originally the 'H' of its discoverer, Sir William Herschel. Television is associated with Uranus, and the first television aerial resembled this symbol.

In *mythology* Uranus (Heaven) was the Greek name for the personification of the night sky. As a planet Uranus was not known to the ancients, being discovered in 1781. Its discovery coincided with *entirely new* developments characteristic of its principle: the Industrial Revolution and a new age of scientific invention and discovery, which set the trends for the later harnessing of electrical and magnetic forces, the aeroplane, radio, television, as well as the increasing independence of the individual and drastic changes in social patterns of behaviour.

Physiologically Uranus seems to be particularly associated with the *sympathetic nervous system*. Disease and disorders connected with the planet's function are of primarily nervous origin, often appearing unexpectedly. Is associated with mental disorders of a very excitable and convulsive nature. Sudden nervous breakdowns, hysteria, abnormal or freak growth, all forms of spasms, cramps, paralysis, palpitation are attributable to Uranus, activated with other factors.

The change of life in both sexes is closely linked with the Moon-Saturn-Uranus cycles: in the early-forties both the progressed Moon and transiting Saturn for the second time, and transiting Uranus for the first time, oppose their respective positions in the natal chart (of each one of us). Moon and Uranus are associated with functional changes, whilst Saturn significantly determines the time scheduled for this critical readjustment of the whole physical organism and Psyche. It is noteworthy that at this stage in life the sympathetic nervous system seems to be more *unstable* than is normal.

The Uranus principle may well correspond to the *pineal body* and *gonads* (sex glands) of the endocrine system. The pineal is thought to be the remnant of a 'third eye' referred to in ancient writings and drawings. Occultists claim it is the source of 'seership' (spiritual vision) and psychic clairvoyance. The pineal is said to be a communicating centre between the brain and the other organs, and tumours in this gland produce accelerated sexual development. Homosexuality and sexual perversions are connected with Uranus.

Psychologically the urge to *deviate from the normal*. When we think of Uranus as the first planet beyond the boundary traced by Saturn's orbit we may see a clue to the symbology of Uranus. It represents a breakaway force from the rigidly controlled normal organism. It is revolt, anarchy, a sudden dramatic flash of genius. It is intuition, an unexpected insight to a yet unborn future design. It may be Nature's way to ensure the creation of entirely new features and disrupt life out of its cyclic rut of accepted order and limitations. Through this disruptive impulse springs originality, creative inspiration, scientific thought, inventiveness, the urge for independence and freedom of expression, image-forming power, altruism, unorthodoxy, rebellious or reformative impulses, free and illicit sexual behaviour, the urge to make drastic changes from the normal. Afflictions to Uranus suggest a tendency for irresponsible, eccentric, violent, perverted, fanatical, depraved, or simply peculiar behaviour.

Uranus is specially associated with the sign Aquarius, and the 11th house.

NEPTUNE

Life-principle: Refinement, through dissolution, subtlety, immateriality, sensitivity.

Symbol: Ψ The trident of the god Neptune. The mind or evolving human spirit (half-circle) transcending the physical (cross). Identified with the chalice of the Holy Grail legends.

In *mythology* Neptune was personified as the Roman god of the sea, Neptunus, identified with the Greek sea-god Poseidon, and the marine diety of the Hindus, Varuna.

One of the most remarkable achievements in *astronomy* was Neptune's discovery. Its first sighting in 1846 was the culmination of many years of speculation and calculation by astronomers in an effort to determine the possible existence of a hypothetical planet that was causing an increasing deviation of Uranus from its predicted course. Astrologically the appearance of Neptune into the consciousness of mankind 'coincided' with a new awareness to matters that have since been found correlative to the Neptune principle in Nature. *Anaesthetics* were introduced into surgical practice; *Mesmerism* had excited attention again, whilst the name of *hypnotism* was first used in 1843; and in America and England the *Spiritualist* movement was born.

Physiologically the Neptune principle seems particularly associated with the *thalamus*, the *spinal canal* and the *nervous and mental processes* generally. The thalamus is a part of the brain from which optic and hearing nerves spring; it has nervous connections with the pituitary gland. In fact, the thalamus has been called the conductor of the pituitary (rhythms of growth) whereby the whole of the endocrine system is coordinated. Botanically thalamus means the receptacle of a flower (think of the Neptune symbol), derived from the Greek *thalamos*, an inner or secret chamber (typically Neptunian). Of similar origins we find *thalassic* means 'of the sea' (Neptune affinity); *thallus*, a vegetable structure from which true roots are absent (symbolised by the sea the Neptune function has no roots materially, is the non-confined, the dissolver of form) which includes algae, fungi and lichens (traditionally associated with Neptune). An afflicted Neptune is invariably found in the charts of those who suffer from mysterious illnesses, severe mental or emotional disturbance, or the incurably insane, and always where there is a deep-rooted neurosis. Neptune's correspondence is with one of the subtlest and most 'refined' forces working within the mind and body of man.

Psychologically the urge through the sensory mechanisms and the most sensitive perceptive faculties to seek experience beyond and detached from all material form and structure. Its function stimulates the nervous and emotional responses to an extreme pitch of sensitivity and excitement. It is an essential link with the 'invisible realms of inspiration' for the brilliant composer and musician, poet, painter, religious leader. It is the subtle and powerful disintegrator, source of hallucinations and hysteria, in the mentally deranged; the link with the spiritual energies outside of man, or with the deceptive forces of the unconscious mind, which create the trance and psychic conditions of spiritual mediums; and is the process working through both hypnotist and hypnotised. It develops impressionability, idealism, artistic sensitivity, unworldliness, day-dreaming, mystical experiences, love of the sea, intensely religious or humanistic feelings. When Neptune is strong in a chart, drugs, sedatives, alcohol should be taken with discretion. Afflictions to Neptune suggest a tendency to woolly-headedness, escapism, self-deception or flagrant dishonesty, impracticality and generally confused and chaotic handling of one's life, vagueness, hypersensitivity, sensationalism, obsessional fears, and risk of poisoning, gassing, drowning. It is the subtle architect of chaos, fantasy, self-disintegration, illusion, and despair through the hidden yet potent forces of the unconscious in ourselves, which tempts escape into degrading drinking and sexual orgies and perversions, neuroses, suicide, homesexuality.

Neptune is specially associated with the sign Pisces, and the 12th house.

PLUTO

Life-principle: Transformative, through elimination, renewal.
Symbol: ♇ Originally the PL of Percival Lowell who made exhaustive calculations of Pluto's probable position, which was discovered by the Lowell Observatory about 14 years after his death.

In *mythology* Pluto was the god of the underworld, called Hades by the Greeks, Pluto or Dis by the Romans, Mantus by the Etruscans, and by various other names in most countries where there was primitive worship of gods who personified the higher and lower natures recognised in man.

Astronomically Pluto is the planet at present furthest from the Sun, though for one period of its orbit it passes within that of Neptune's. Astrologically, as the outermost planet known to man, it represents the limits of his present stage of consciousness. Pluto's orbit is very eccentric. So much that it takes only 13 years to go through some signs, as seen from the Earth, but as much as 32 years through others. This tiny, remote planet can swing to a height more than three times that of the Moon's maximum above the ecliptic, and plunge to a similar extent below the ecliptic. This seems symbolical of the great heights or fearful depths to which man can rise or fall through the function associated with Pluto. Its discovery in 1930 corresponded with the climax of the racketeering and gangsterdom era in the United States, the 1920's and 1930's period which saw the birth of dictatorships, development of atomic power, the greatest economic depression the world had known. Pluto, Neptune and Uranus were always associated with a principle within man before each was discovered, but it would seem that man's initial awareness to each synchronised with a new awakening to those impulses they correspond to.

Physiologically Pluto seems to be associated with the creative and regenerative forces in the body, involving cell-formation and the reproductive function. This does not mean Pluto alone is connected with these, but that it would seem to correspond to an essential mediating role for the use of these physical re-creative forces for the mental processes. Thus, correspondence with the gonads, and mental processes, and afflictions to Pluto suggest possible disorders or disease through these.

Psychologically Pluto corresponds to a process of subterranean activities deep within the unconscious, like the deepest roots of a tree which are essential for bringing to the surface necessary elements both for nourishment and for release through the leaves. It is a dual role of elimination and renewal, physically and psychologically. Its process forces 'out into the open', into consciousness, a problem, the root cause of a neurosis, or a revealing truth, that has been long hidden and yet unconsciously agitating the mind, which the system can no longer contain in its existing form. It has to be completely eliminated or transformed. Pluto corresponds to the critical phase in the cycle of life-force, or any process or activity, where death or the bringing to an end is inevitable, that rebirth or a new beginning can occur. It is associated with the forces which initiate colossal business enterprises and combines, mass hysteria, mob lynchings, political blood-purges. Psychologically it is the Whole Self in opposition to a particular discordant or unnecessary feature. An afflicted Pluto suggests possible 'difficulty in elimination', hence suppression of unpleasant feelings with consequent risk of obsessional and neurotic conditions, and in severe cases probable eruptive outbursts of violence or self-destruction.

Pluto is specially associated with the sign Scorpio, and the 8th house.

Recommended reading

My *The Planets and Human Behaviour* is recommended to the reader who wishes to gain a broader and deeper understanding of the Sun, Moon and each planet in terms of their correlation with basic psychological drives and traits.

4

The 12 signs: psychological types

In the previous chapter it was said that the basic life-principles in man (planets) find expression through the signs (correlated with the Earth-Sun interaction). The signs have only a mythological association with the constellations bearing their names. This theory that the signs correlate with the Earth's orbit of the Sun may seem far-fetched, but you will be able to find out for yourself that these 12 areas of the ecliptic *do* correspond to characteristics of predetermined types, and that the correspondence could be one of synchronisation on a time-space basis of similar principles which both the Earth-Sun magnetic fields and human life are subject to.

I will refer to these areas of the ecliptic in the traditional way, as *signs*, but I want you to think of these as 12 psychological *types*, 12 basic *attitudes*, 12 basic ways of human expression.

You must realise that you and I contain in our total make-up the ingredients or potential characteristics of *all* the 12 signs. Just as we contain the life-principles associated with *each* planet. Because, let us say, you may have the Sun in Aries, a Leo Ascendant, and Moon in Virgo, does not mean you are composed only of the substance of these three signs because they happen to be (as an astrologer would say) prominent or strong in your chart. The characteristics of these three signs would be very evident in the way you respond to life and express yourself, whilst the other nine types of attitude would be much *less* evident, some altogether latent and *unawakened*. But each of the 12 would be a part of your unconscious self. The signs containing planets, or on the Ascendant[1] or Midheaven, indicate the more awakened or conscious features. The planets correspond to focal points of energy, functions developing consciousness: the signs through which these

[1] See Chapter 7.

points are focused indicate the characteristic modes of self-expression most naturally employed.

A common mistake in astrology is to think the same way about a planet and the sign it 'rules' as though they were identical factors. For instance, the planet Mars and the sign Aries are both traditionally factors of 'energetic expression'. But Mars, being a planet or life-principle, is a *source of energy*; Aries, because representing *an attitude of urgency and objectivity*, provides a suitable *channel* for this energy to be expressed through.

Traditionally the 12 signs or types are classified under three important groupings. These will help you to learn the essential quality and attitude of each sign more clearly.

Group 1: **Positivity and negativity** (see Figure 4)

Keywords:

> *Positive:* Self-expressive; spontaneous; extraverted.
> *Negative:* Self-repressive; passive; introverted.

The signs (starting from Aries) are alternately positive and negative. Positive are odd-numbered signs. Negative is not to be thought of as inferior in any way to positive in the sense used here. Positive implies a tendency to *extraversion*, negative implies a tendency to *introversion*, as you will fully understand as you read Chapter 18. Thus there is a tendency for the positive signs to be more frequently self-expressive and less passive in their reactions, and for the negative signs to be more frequently self-repressive and less outgoing and spontaneous. The positive category are of the Fire and Air elements, the negative are of the Earth and Water elements.

Group 2: **The triplicities (or elements)** (see Figure 4)

Keywords:

> *Fire:* Energetic; assertive (Aries, Leo, Sagittarius)
> *Earth:* Practical; restrained (Taurus, Virgo, Capricorn)
> *Air:* Communicative; mentally active (Gemini, Libra, Aquarius)
> *Water:* Emotional; intuitive (Cancer, Scorpio, Pisces)

These are basic elements in man, recognised by the earliest of astrologers. The three signs associated with each element have a common basis for harmony *through* this element, as when set in the chart they are united by the trine (120°) aspect. This four-fold division has an interesting resemblance to Jung's four types: feeling (Fire), sensation (Earth),

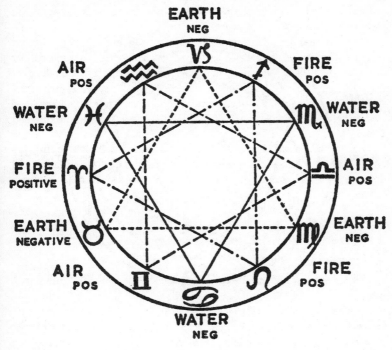

FIGURE 4
The Triplicities (Elements)

thinking (Air), and intuition (Water), but this is not a clear-cut correspondence. The keywords given above should be carefully memorised.

Group 3: **The quadruplicities (or qualities)** (see Figure 5)

Keywords:

Cardinal: Enterprising (Aries, Cancer, Libra, Capricorn)
Fixed: Intense; steadfast (Taurus, Leo, Scorpio, Aquarius)
Mutable: Adaptable; variable (Gemini, Virgo, Sagittarius, Pisces)

Each category of four signs have a common factor or quality, and yet each sign when set in the chart is at right-angles (90° square aspect) or opposition (180° aspect) to each other. Hence, people in whose charts these signs are prominent would possess a basic quality of expression common to each other, but this quality in each sign would be

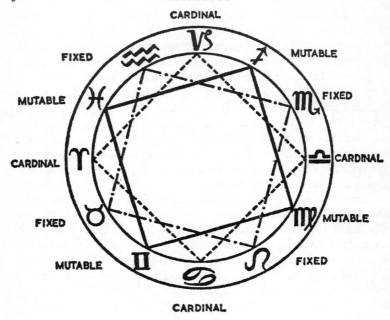

FIGURE 5
The Quadruplicities (Qualities)

applied differently (because the make-up of each is of a different element) and therefore suggests an underlying source of stress or conflict between them. For instance, we find the Cardinal quality is in Aries which is *Fire*, Cancer which is *Water*, Libra which is *Air*, and Capricorn which is *Earth*. Thus, these have a common factor of enterprise, but with Aries this will be applied *energetically* and *assertively* (Fire element); with Cancer it would best be applied through their *intuitive* faculty and the strength and sensitivity of their *emotional* nature (Water element); with Libra they will prove most enterprising through *mental* and *communicative* activities (Air element); and with Capricorn their enterprising ability will be expressed through *practical* endeavours, and where with Aries there would be no thought for risks involved, with Capricorn there would be an essential *restraint* (Earth element), and any risk would be a 'calculated risk'.

You can also understand the basic structure of each sign from another angle. Each of the four elements has three modes of expression: Cardinal, Fixed, Mutable (motion, inertia, and changeableness or adaptability). Thus, the Air element in each one of us of *communicative* and *mental activity* will through Gemini be of a Mutable quality; through Libra be of a Cardinal quality; through Aquarius be of a Fixed quality.

You have been shown in Chapter 3 how the life-principle connected with each planet appears to represent archetypal forces functioning within man and Nature, which the ancients personified as gods. The Signs of the Zodiac have also been associated with archetypal forces, and their names seemingly derive from primitive man's intuitional experience of the characteristics of these forces, which we now recognise as basic and necessarily complementary impulses and behaviour within us all in lesser and greater degree.

In individual cases certain of these signs are strongly emphasised, and so we each express ourselves in a typical manner according to the *type* of characteristics connected with the signs emphasised in our own chart. *But no one person will ever be wholly representative of one type.* This is where astrological interpretation becomes an art. First you must learn the characteristics of each of the 12 types, but when you come to interpret a personal chart you must know how to blend the contrasting features into a balanced caricature of the person concerned, and recognise which are the strongest characteristics to emphasise.

Physiological correspondences to the 12 types (signs)

Starting with Aries, the first sign, and the head, the signs correspond to consecutive regions of the physical body right down to the feet, connected with Pisces the 12th sign.

Symbol	Sign	Region
♈	Aries	head as a whole
♉	Taurus	throat and neck
♊	Gemini	lungs, chest
♋	Cancer	breasts, stomach
♌	Leo	heart
♍	Virgo	abdomen, intestines
♎	Libra	kidneys, lumbar
♏	Scorpio	genitals, bladder, rectum
♐	Sagittarius	hips, thighs
♑	Capricorn	knees
♒	Aquarius	calves, ankles
♓	Pisces	feet

Interesting and helpful correspondences can be traced through the relationship of parts of the anatomy to the psychological types, which indicate the discipline of the whole body to natural laws, and the inter-relationship of each part to all other parts. Pathological tendencies of the various types (signs) can be associated with corresponding parts of the body, and fully bear out accepted medical knowledge. With his astrological keys the astrologer can invariably diagnose the psychological disturbance causing a particular physical sickness, and vice versa. Naturally the astrologer, if he has no medical training, has to be extremely cautious in his diagnoses. Space does not permit me to do justice to what I have said here, and the serious reader will extend his studies through other books.

One example could be given, however, indicating the *antipathy* of particular signs. Take the Fixed signs (see Figure 5). There are polarities between Leo-Aquarius, and Taurus-Scorpio. These form a cross. Heart trouble (Leo) can have reflex effects in the ankles (Aquarius). Likewise there is a recognised polarity between throat glandular conditions (Taurus) and sexual disturbances (Scorpio), and vice versa. Consider the change of voice (larynx) corresponding to the male sex glandular change at puberty. There is *sympathy* between the parts of the body related through the Triplicity classifications (see Figure 4) which you can confirm for yourself.

Keyword formula for interpreting the function of the signs

The principle or nature of a planet will function through the signs as follows:

Through			
	Aries	♈	objectively, urgently
	Taurus	♉	productively, enduringly
	Gemini	♊	adaptively, variably
	Cancer	♋	defensively, sensitively
	Leo	♌	powerfully, impressively
	Virgo	♍	analytically, critically
	Libra	♎	relatedly, harmoniously
	Scorpio	♏	penetratingly, intensely
	Sagittarius	♐	extensively, freely
	Capricorn	♑	rationally, prudently
	Aquarius	♒	detachedly, unconventionally
	Pisces	♓	nebulously, impressionably

As was said regards the planetary keywords, these are suggested to give a *central idea* of the signs.

In the following explanation of the 12 types or signs the basic structure of each is composed of the blending of its particular classification within the three important groupings of human nature: Positivity and Negativity; the Triplicities or Elements; the Quadruplicities or Qualities.

It will be noticed that the first six signs express, in a broad sense, a particularly *personal* application; whereas the last six express a desire to enter more into experience with other people. The last six are, as it were, the projection or rising above the mere personal interest of their opposite numbers.

The characteristics of a particular sign will be emphasised not only when it contains the Sun but when it is the Ascendant or Midheaven, or is strengthened by containing planets.

ARIES

Traditionally the first sign of the zodiac.
Associated with Mars and the sphere of life of the 1st house.
Classification: Cardinal-Fire; Positive.
Symbol: The Ram. ♈

Cardinal-fire and positive implies: Essentially self-expressive, energetic and assertive, with qualities of enterprise and spontaneity. Extraverted.

Keyword definition. Develops an *objective* attitude expressing *urgency*, associated with an urge to *project* oneself energetically and actively into life.

The Ram (♈). The Aries symbol resembles the horns of the ram, and symbolically this thrusting, aggressive leader of the flock, always ready to accept a challenge to its prowess and masculinity, is identified with the Aries type.

Characteristic Aries type. Is impulsive, self-assertive, restless, always wanting quick results and giving the impression of urgency. Develops initiative, enterprise, a pioneering and adventurous spirit. Seems naturally courageous and fearless. Attitude is 'me first', rather than being naturally individualistic. Frank and direct. A go-getter, freedom-lover.

Mentally quick-thinking, quick-witted, though not reflective or philosophical. Can conceive the start and finish of an enterprise, but overlooks the details or possible snags that lie between.

In love is passionate, not particularly tactful or refined. Strong sexual feelings.

Faults: selfish, impatient, argumentative, quick-tempered, foolhardy, aggressive, insensitive to feelings of others, brusque, rude, bullying, too quick to be thorough, over-impulsive and restless, thoughtless, over-optimistic.

Ideal vocational activities: as leader, boss; where initiative and pioneering spirit needed; with plenty of physical exercise; in competitive, challenging, crusading enterprises. No good where noise and bustle objected to, where patience and steady plodding and cooperation are necessary. As soldiers, surgeons, engineers, mechanics, professional sportsmen and women, dentists, explorers.

Psychologically the primitive urge to project oneself energetically, actively, objectively, combatively, sexually.

Physiological: the head as a whole, symbolic of the desire to be at the head of things, first; reflex association with the kidneys (through Libra). Tendency for severe headaches, neuralgia, sunstroke, inflammations, head injuries. Impulsive nature brings risk of accidents, haemorrhage.

TAURUS

Traditionally the second sign of the zodiac.
Associated with Venus and the sphere of life of the 2nd house.
Classification: Fixed-Earth; Negative.
Symbol: The Bull. ♉

Fixed-earth and negative implies: Essentially restrained, self-repressive, passive and intense, with qualities of practicality and steadfastness. Introverted.

Keyword definition. Develops a *productive* attitude expressing *enduringness*, associated with an urge for *organic relatedness, security and material sustenance.*

The Bull (♉). The Taurean symbol resembles the full face and horns of the bull, and symbolically this powerfully built, possessive animal, unflinching in attack when enraged, is identified with the Taurean type.

Characteristic Taurean type. Is practical, reliable, steadfast. Must have security. Good powers of endurance and patience. Instinctively conserves, withholds, needs to possess. Sound sense of material values, art, beauty, harmony. Love of good food, luxuries, comfort. Productive, industrious, cautious nature. Fixed ways and opinions, strong feelings.

Mentally stable, methodical, deliberate, constructive. Unoriginal;

thought-processes follow accepted and reliable patterns. Can be a bit of a bore and too heavy.

In love is very affectionate, sensual, instinctively aware of the useful power of their body sexually. Possessive.

Faults: too-possessive, self-indulgent, stubborn, gets in a rut, stodgy, self-centred, grasping, resentful of contradiction, slavishly adherent to routine.

Ideal vocational activities: position of trust and responsibility; where sense of material values and practicality, artistic and productive flair, can be exercised, without urgency, risk of sudden changes or insecurity; where perseverance, patience, economy are required; a routine job with the reward of a pension at the end. As builders, farmers, bankers, Civil Servants, industrialists, architects, surveyors, accountants, auctioneers, economists, jewellers, artists – especially singers, sculptors.

Psychologically the primitive urge for organic relatedness, security, material sustenance.

Physiological: throat and neck, symbolic of the connective, supporting function of Taurus. Thyroid gland, ears. Reflex association with the sexual glands (through Scorpio). Tendency to throat infections, goitre, over-weight, ear-ache, genital or womb trouble.

GEMINI

Traditionally the third sign of the zodiac.
Associated with Mercury and the sphere of life of the 3rd house.
Classification: Mutable-Air; Positive.
Symbol: The Twins. ♊

Mutable-air and positive implies: Essentially communicative, self-expressive and mentally active, with qualities of adaptability, variability and spontaneity. Extraverted.

Keyword definition. Develops an *adaptive* attitude expressing *variableness*, associated with an urge to *adjust* oneself to environment, and *communicate* with others.

The Twins (♊). The Geminian symbol resembles the Roman numeral II, and symbolises the duality and 'never two minds alike' nature.

Characteristic Geminian type. Is adaptable, communicative, versatile. Incessantly on the go, restless, inquisitive, liking variety and change, contriving ingenious methods for transmitting anything from here to there. In this way he is the ideal middle-man, mediator. Nervously-excitable, inconsistent, witty, chatty, never dull.

Mentally agile and intelligent; the positive type an orator or teacher, the negative type a gossiper or crafty spiv. Learns easily, good at languages. The chattering, imitative, restless monkey has been suggested as the Geminian symbol!

In love tends to be light-hearted, fickle, coolly affectionate, flirtatious, unemotional, likely to have 'a second string to his bow'.

Faults: superficiality, lack of continuity, two-faced, diffuseness, inconsisten*, cunning, dissipates nervous energy.

Ideal vocational activities: where the brain or intellect can be exercised to the fullest, and there is opportunity to do, learn, and see new things, make changes, travel, continually make fresh personal contacts. Clever and skilful at light manual work, averse to hard labour! As an agent, commercial traveller, news reporter, clerk, shorthand-typist, secretary, lecturer, teacher, writer, broker, merchant, solicitor, and in transport, printing and publishing.

Psychologically the primitive urge for adjusting oneself to and being aware of environment, and communicating awareness to others.

Physiological: respiratory system, nervous system, hands, arms. Reflex association with the hips and sciatic nerves (through Sagittarius). Tendency to nervous diseases and exhaustion, rheumatism, pulmonary disorders, as bronchitis, pneumonia, pleurisy, asthma.

CANCER

Traditionally the fourth sign of the zodiac.
Associated with the Moon and the sphere of life of the 4th house.
Classification: Cardinal-Water; Negative.
Symbol: The Crab. ♋

Cardinal-water and negativity implies: Essentially emotional, intuitive, self-repressing and passive, yet of an enterprising quality. Introverted.

Keyword definition. Develops a *defensive* attitude expressing *sensitiveness*, associated with an urge to *protect* and to *nourish*.

The Crab (♋). The Cancerian symbol resembles the human breasts, symbolising the desire to nourish and protect, traits and physical glands identified with the Cancerian type. Also suggests the crab's claws, symbolising the indrawing, clinging-to nature; and this creature with its exterior protective crust of shell, and soft, sensitive interior, is typical of the Cancerian.

Characteristic Cancerian type. Is highly sensitive, easily hurt within, but outwardly giving the impression of impenetrable self-assurance and toughness. Resourceful, tenaciously protective and loyal to their family. Instinctive clannishness and patriotism. Need security, and a womb-like shelter to withdraw into whilst restoring self-confidence. Sympathetic, imaginative, sentimental, moody, reserved. Loves to collect things. Instinctive outgoing urge conflicts with the emotional and indrawn nature, that can only be resolved by regulation to these rhythms which are essential to the function of this type. Artistic inclination.

Mentally shrewd, intuitive, receptive, retentive. Good memory. Very impressionable to psychic influences, and apt to let emotions colour the thoughts.

In love tends to be romantic, sentimental, very clinging and tender. Maternal instincts strong with women, protective instincts with men. Touchy. Vulnerable to sensual stimulation.

Faults: very touchy, moody, inclined to self-pity, timid, untidy, unstable, easily flattered, too clannish, harbour slights, sensuous, inferiority complex, over-emotional.

Ideal vocational activities: where the emotional energies and sensitive nature can be constructively employed and not aggravated by discordant conditions; looking after others; where the shrewd, economising abilities have value; to do with the sea, liquids. As nurses, estate agents, archaeologists, nursery gardeners, hoteliers, brewers, publicans.

Psychologically the primitive urge to protect and to nourish, especially the feminine desire to receive into the womb and to possess.

Physiological: the breasts, female reproductive system, stomach, alimentary system generally. Reflex association with the skin and knees (through Capricorn). Tendency to digestive and gastric troubles, dropsy, womb afflictions, breast disorders and growths.

LEO

Traditionally the fifth sign of the zodiac.
Associated with the Sun and the sphere of life of the 5th house.
Classification: Fixed-Fire; Positive.
Symbol: The Lion. ♌

Fixed-fire and positive implies: Essentially self-expressive, energetic, assertive, with qualities of intenseness, steadfastness and spontaneity. Extraverted.

Keyword definition. Develops a *powerful* attitude expressing *impressiveness*, associated with an urge for authority.

The Lion (♌). The Leonian symbol resembles the lion's mane, and symbolically this 'king of the beasts' with its power, its roar, its regal bearing, is identified with the Leo type.

Characteristic Leo type. The basic conflict in the nature is indicated by the active Fire element and the static Fixed quality. Through the latter it is essential this type *controls* the self-assertive element which can force upon others the great sense of pride and authority and become overbearing, dominating. Too much Fixed quality is equally overbearing. Is generous, warm-hearted, a born leader, enthusiastic, dignified, broad-minded, outspoken, a good organiser, loves doing things in a 'big way' and can't be bothered with details. Strong sense of the dramatic. Usually very self-assured. Love of pleasure.

Mentally seeks powerful, forthright expression. Intellectually inclined. Generalises, looks for the broad, overall pattern.

In love has powerful and sincere feelings, is wholehearted and generous and endeavours to bring sunshine into the loved one's life.

Faults: overbearing, too fixed in opinions, intolerant, autocratic, conceited, pompous, bombastic, sensual, snobbish, self-appraising, patronising.

Ideal vocational activities: where the natural qualities of leadership and powerful self-assurance can be fully applied; as manager, director, chairman, social organiser, overseer; where the generous, sunny, warm-hearted, creative, artistic, reliable, strong-principled qualities can be naturally developed and encouraged. As actor, actress.

Psychologically the primitive urge for power. Primary source of the power-complex.

Physiological: heart, symbolically the central source of power of an organism. The dorsal region of spine, back generally. Reflex association with the circulatory system and ankles (through Aquarius). Tendency to cardiac trouble, spinal afflictions.

VIRGO

Traditionally the sixth sign of the zodiac.
Associated with Mercury and the sphere of life of the 6th house.
Classification: Mutable-Earth; Negative.
Symbol: The Virgin. ♍

Mutable-earth and negative implies: Essentially self-repressive, passive, restrained, with qualities of practicality, adaptability and variableness. Introverted.

Keyword definition. Develops an *analytical* attitude expressing *criticalness*, associated with an urge for *efficiency* and *perfection*.

The Virgin (♍). The only feminine figure in the zodiac, depicted holding an ear of wheat, symbol of fertility. Throughout the ancient world she was worshipped as the earth-goddess, identified with Isis, Ishtar, Persephone, Ceres and many others, even later with the Virgin Mary.

Characteristic Virgoan type. Is critical, discriminating, practical, evaluating life by facts and logic. Must analyse, take to pieces, sift the minutest details for the key to their significance to the whole. Theirs is an unconsciously motivated process of grinding and separating material into assimilative, digestible particles, that only the pure essence shall become part of themselves. Hence, thorough, methodical, conscientious, precise. Interest in hygiene, cleanliness. Reserved.

Mentally intelligent, shrewd, discerning, critical, practical rather than abstract, able to assimilate great detail. Is the scholastic mind, dealing in logical subtleties. Easy to educate.

In love has either a strictly conventional approach, of refined manners, modest and well-tempered display of emotion and affection, or tend to exercise their love of techniques, and their analytical mental energies, in the most harmless sexual idiosyncrasies or ingeniously contrived perversions. This must be understood as a *tendency* that may only be evident where there is lack of control shown elsewhere in the chart, or over-emphasis, and no doubt results from the instinctive desire for 'purity' at the expense of normal emotional and sensual expression.

Faults: hypercritical, pedantic, fastidious, hypocritical, interfering, too modest, suppression of emotions and feelings, over-specialisation, worrying.

Ideal vocational activities: where discriminative, analytical, assimilative abilities can be encouraged and exercised. Routine and very detailed work. Is a born 'server'. As a teacher, psychologist, technologist, nursing and all types of work connected with the health and hygiene of the community, analytical scientist, statistician, accountant, secretary, critic, inspector.

Psychologically the primitive urge for efficiency, perfection. This is the essence of the Virgin symbol. Not virginity in the specifically sexual sense, but the need to develop techniques to avoid waste of one's energies, to ensure maximum efficiency, and to be 'pure' and free from the influence of others. This is the self-analytical type and the perfectionist, but also, negatively, the hypochondriac and pest of both doctors and psychoanalysts.

Physiological: abdominal region, intestines, spleen, central nervous system. Reflex association with the feet (through Pisces). Tendency to intestinal complaints, ulcers (especially through worrying), appendicitis, peritonitis, nervous disorders.

LIBRA

Traditionally the seventh sign of the zodiac.
Associated with Venus and the sphere of life of the 7th house.
Classification: Cardinal-Air; Positive.
Symbol: The Scales. ♎

Cardinal-air and positive implies: Essentially self-expressive, communicative, mentally active, with qualities of enterprise and spontaneity. Extraverted.

Keyword definition. Develops an attitude of *relatedness* expressing *harmony*, associated with an urge for *unity* with others.

The Scales (♎). The only inanimate object among the signs, its symbol resembling scales, a balance. Typical of the Libran who is always 'weighing life in the balance', bringing people together and comparing them. Essentially, too, they seek in or through others for balancing qualities that are lacking in themselves. It typifies their frequent indecisiveness, weighing the pros and cons too long that in the end they often go from one extreme to the other.

Characteristic Libran type. Is charming, kind, easy-going. Natural desire to be diplomatic and cooperative. Will do anything for 'peace and harmony', and is completely unsettled in an environment of discord and conflict. Good evaluation of harmony, art, beauty, form. Is idealistic, at heart a perfectionist. Often called 'Lazy Libra', but this apparent laziness can be indecision and dependence on others to shake them from their idealistic dreams.

Mentally intelligent and capable of very balanced judgment, but inclined to indecision, easily influenced by the opinions of others. Their thinking is along cheerful, optimistic, compromising lines.

In love they have achieved something of their ideal and though they may recognise even the smallest failing in their loved one they must not argue over it for fear of 'disturbing the balance'. Romantic, sentimental. Frequently a 'marriage of minds' than an 'earthy mating of sexes'. But there is the shallow, flirtatious type!

Faults: indecision, too easy-going, untidy, frivolous, 'sit on the fence', changeable, lack of confidence, too soft.

Ideal vocational activities: where the human factor and relationships are essential considerations; in congenial, harmonious environment, away from noise and coarseness. As an artist, poet, and where the sense of harmony and balance can be developed. As a diplomat, connoisseur, beauty specialist, hairdresser, valuer, social worker, staff welfare officer, hostess. In millinery, textiles, cosmetics.

Psychologically the primitive urge for unity and relatedness with others. Strong sense of social duty, and the need to conform to an ideal pattern of community life. An underlying sense of personal inadequacy sometimes leads to misunderstanding through doing what they *think* is expected of them.

Physiological: kidneys, lumbar region, symbolical through the kidneys of 'weighing and eliminating what is unwanted'. Reflex association with the head, particularly eyes (through Aries). Tendency to kidney complaints, lumbago.

SCORPIO

Traditionally the eighth sign of the zodiac.
Associated with Pluto and Mars and the sphere of life of the 8th house.
Classification: Fixed-Water; Negative.
Symbol: The Scorpion and the Eagle. ♏

Fixed-water and negative implies: Essentially self-repressive, passive, emotional, intuitive, with qualities of intenseness and steadfastness. Introverted.

Keyword definition. Develops a *penetrating* attitude expressing *intenseness*, associated with an urge to identify oneself with *one's source*.

The Scorpion and the Eagle (♏). The Scorpio symbol vaguely resembles the legs and tail of the scorpion, which is essentially a creature of darkness, secretive, hiding in the shadows. Its sting is out of all proportion to its size and strikes when least expected. Throughout the ancient world Scorpio was cursed as evil. The Mayas called it the 'Sign of the death-god'. In the Euphrates Valley, where it probably originated, the sign represented a monster, half scorpion, half man. The human half belonged to the upper regions, the animal half to the underworld, Hades. Later, the Eagle corresponded to this upper region, representing the power within man, *through the Scorpio function*, to rise above the temptations of his lower nature. Scorpio, and its natural house, the 8th, have always been associated with the mystic life force in its critical phases of transformation: birth, the sexual act, death. But particularly with the sexual act and death. Both imply a rebirth.

Characteristic Scorpionic type. There is an intensity of expression, of thinking and feeling, that springs from an inner depth. It may be seen as strength of will, a magnetic quality, the penetrating eyes, the passion and power of conviction. It is not always evident, yet it is there, subtly concealed perhaps like the scorpion, a power as potent yet restrained until ready to strike as the little creature's sting. There is a power-house of emotional energy that needs to be harnessed constructively. In each one of us this is the feeling part most intimately and mystically involved with the regenerative process, through which we were originally transformed from a single cell united by our parents, through which we ourselves re-create life, and through which, inevitably, we must face the ultimate transformation of death. Little wonder the Scorpio type is subtle, secretive, purposeful, takes experiences deep within himself, seems even stronger in his silence, whose essential characteristics have been identified with the intense spiritual fervour of the mystic, the ice-cold self-control of the surgeon, the aggressive brutality of dangerous criminals, the courage of great soldiers, and with the passion and consummating joy of lovers!

Mentally has strong reasoning power, is secretive, imaginative, intuitive, capable of skilful and penetrating thought. Analytical, keenly perceptive.

In love is passionate, often extremely jealous. Strong sexual feelings.

Faults: brooding resentment, jealousy, destructive, stubborn, secretive, suspicious, vindictive, capable of deliberate cruelty.

Ideal vocational activities: research work, analysing, solving mysteries, dealing with realities rather than trivialities. As surgeon, soldier, detective, psychologist, undertaker, physicist, butcher, scientist, lawyer, occult investigator, spiritualist healer.

Psychologically the primitive urge to identify oneself with one's source. Primarily an unconscious motive that is sought through the sexual function, personal sense of power, desire to penetrate to the roots of life and uncover its mysteries, the urge to be more than oneself. It is sex as a *personal problem*, the urge to be as one, locked at the roots, with another human being, in an ecstasy and mystical experience of self-forgetfulness. Scorpio symbolises the root communion of all men.

Physiological: genitals, bladder, urethra, rectum. Reflex association with the throat and nasal bones (through Taurus). Tendency to genital troubles, venereal disease, rupture, renal stones, nasal catarrh, polypi, adenoids.

It would be opportune to mention here the several associations with the sexual function. Venus and Libra symbolise the urge to unite as a process of human love, and has its natural expression through sex; Mars is the sensual and energetic stimulant for this process working through the whole physical aspects of sex; Scorpio is the urge to be united with the essential identifying factor within all men and women, and inevitably involves stimulation of the sexual glands; Taurus, as Scorpio's polarity, responds to sex stimulation by a normally healthy desire for sensual gratification; Pluto's role is not too clear, but seems to be vitally linked with the regenerative forces as a mediating factor for transforming procreative sexual energy into mental energy.

SAGITTARIUS

Traditionally the ninth sign of the zodiac.
Associated with Jupiter and the sphere of life of the 9th house.
Classification: Mutable-Fire; Positive.
Symbol: The Centaur with Bow and Arrow. ♐

Mutable-fire and positive implies: Essentially self-expressive, energetic, assertive, with qualities of adaptability, variableness and spontaneity. Extraverted.

Keyword definition. Develops an *extensive* attitude expressing *freedom*, associated with an urge to *explore* beyond one's *known environment*.

The Centaur with bow and arrow (♐). The Sagittarius symbol resembles the bow with the arrow drawn ready to be aimed by the Centaur or Archer, who is pictorially depicted as the upper part of man upon the lower parts of a horse. The dual creature implies one with the speed and power of the horse and the brain and potential wisdom of man. Symbolic of the far-reaching, free-ranging, restless and idealistic aims of the typical Sagittarian impulse.

Characteristic Sagittarian type. Seeks space, freedom, opportunity through which to range and aspire to the highest of ambitions, physically and mentally. Is optimistic, sincere, frank. Expresses the Geminian versatility and mental activity expanded and projected more deeply and widely and philosophically. Loves sport and natural pursuits, exploring, adventure. Idealistic, foresighted, jovial, benevolent, with religious and moralising tendencies.

Mentally intellectually-inclined, open-minded, deep thinker, good judgment, outspoken, an interpreter and translator rather than inventor. Seeks new dimensions of thinking.

In love is ardent, sincere, conventional, but must feel free.

Faults: extremist, extravagant, tactless, boastful, inconsiderate, exaggerating, careless, too moralising, restless, a 'playboy' type.

Ideal vocational activities: where the far-sighted, free-ranging, ambitious and versatile qualities can be exercised and developed. In the Church, Law, as interpreter, philosopher. Social administration, intellectual or sporting pursuits. With animals, especially horses and dogs. As scholar, Civil Servant, explorer, traveller, coach, promoter, teacher, politician.

Psychologically the primitive urge to explore beyond one's immediate and known environment. Associated with the freedom-impulse, desire to expand the consciousness. The need to judge, interpret, translate, and formulate laws; to understand, as distinct from just knowing and accepting on face value.

Physiological: hips, thighs, sciatic nerves. Reflex association with the lungs and bronchial region (through Gemini). Tendency to hip diseases, sciatica, rheumatic and pulmonary complaints.

CAPRICORN

Traditionally the tenth sign of the zodiac.
Associated with Saturn and the sphere of life of the 10th house.
Classification: Cardinal-Earth; Negative.
Symbol: The Goat. ♑

Cardinal-earth and negative implies: Essentially self-repressive, passive, restrained, with qualities of enterprise and practicality. Introverted.

Keyword definition. Develops a *rational* attitude expressing *prudence*, associated with an urge to conform to *disciplined* behaviour.

The Goat (♑). The symbol is a distorted resemblance of the original symbol of a goat with a curling fish's tail called Capricornus by the Chaldeans. Has been identified with various mythical 'culture gods' who came from the sea (symbolising the unconscious) to teach man the ways of civilisation, to which they returned at night.

Characteristic Capricornian type. Is patient, persevering, cautious, methodical, resourceful. Inborn ability to bear hardship, frustration, because their nature is conditioned to the necessity for discipline, self-containment, and a serious, responsible attitude to life. Prudence is their keynote: to plan, carefully, coolly, deliberately for the achievement of ambitions. They are prepared to plod on, grinding slowly and surely like the mills of God, with conscientious, dutiful, punctilious concentration and industry.

Mentally cool and calculating, exacting, rationalising, severe.

In love is equally cool and calculating, conservative of affection, cautious, modest, faithful, serious.

Faults: selfish, narrow-minded, too severe and exacting, cruel, unfeeling, critical, miserly, pessimistic, a 'wet blanket', unnecessary worrying, too conventional.

Ideal vocational activities: where the patient, economising, resourceful, responsible, unemotional qualities can be exercised and developed. Where they can establish authority, constructive systems of production and administration, for the benefit of the community or a business. As scientist, manager, headmaster, engineer, Civil Servant, mathematician, farmer, politician, builder.

Psychologically the primitive urge to conform to disciplined behaviour: hence, to construct orderly and resourceful communal patterns. The instinctive need for self-sufficiency, to experience life factually, as a calculable, purposeful process.

Physiological: knees, skin. Reflex association with the digestive system (through Cancer). Tendency to skin rashes and disorders, knee trouble, digestive upsets through over-acidity – often through worrying and suppression of emotions and feelings.

AQUARIUS

Traditionally the eleventh sign of the zodiac.

Associated with Uranus and Saturn and the sphere of life of the 11th house.

Classification: Fixed-Air; Positive.

Symbol: The Water-Carrier. ♒

Fixed-air and positive implies: Essentially self-expressive, communicative, mentally active, with qualities of intenseness, steadfastness and spontaneity. Extraverted.

Keyword definition. Develops a *detached* attitude expressing *unconventionality*, associated with an urge to identify oneself with the *progressive* aims of the community.

The Water-Carrier (♒). The symbol resembles two ripples of water or the conducting waves of light or electricity. Water symbolises intuition, and Aquarius being an Air sign (reasoning intelligence) represents the common factor that must link all men into the Brotherhood of Man through understanding, the blending of intuition and reasoning intelligence creative of mental enlightenment.

Characteristic Aquarian type. Has strong ideals, humanitarian feelings, originality, and is a progressive thinker. Puts intense energy into a cause, but can be dogmatic and allow adherence to their own (often revolutionary and unorthodox) opinions to detach them from truths. Scientifically inclined, artistic, unpredictable, friendly, attracted to the unusual.

Mentally intuitive, intelligent; usually an intellectual bias, full of reformative ideas. Imaginative, broadminded, inventive. Ability to synthesise.

In love wants to be faithful, but the independent nature and dispassionate, detached manner can lead to broken hearts.

Faults: perverse, eccentric, cranky, fanatically unconventional, touchy, rebellious, rudely tactless, lack of personal integrity and principle, too detached, erratic.

Ideal vocational activities: where the intuitive, progressive thinking, fertile mental qualities can be exercised and developed, especially in group work rather than that involving personal factors, perhaps of a reformative nature. Observing, recording truth. As a scientist, photographer, radiographer, writer, broadcaster, psychologist, astrologer, publisher. To do with electricity, electronics, aviation, radio and television, social welfare, general technical trades.

Psychologically the primitive urge to identify oneself with the progressive aims of the community. The impulse for reform and the establishment of human rights, on a social and not individual basis.

Physiological: limbs from knees to ankles, circulatory system. Reflex association with the heart (through Leo). Tendency to varicose veins, sprained ankle, circulatory and cardiac disorders.

PISCES

Traditionally the twelfth sign of the zodiac.

Associated with Neptune and Jupiter and the sphere of life of the 12th house.

Classification: Mutable-Water; Negative.

Symbol: The Fishes.)(

Mutable-water and negative implies: Essentially self-repressive, passive, emotional, with qualities of intuitiveness, adaptability and variableness. Introverted.

Keyword definition. Develops a *nebulous* attitude expressing *impressionableness*, associated with an urge to *transcend the material*.

The Fishes ()(). The symbol represents two fishes joined together and pulling in reverse directions, typical of the dual and vacillating nature of the Piscean type. There are numerous references in the New Testament to these fishes, and the positive Piscean characteristics are embodied in the teaching of Jesus, essentially universal love, self-renunciation, service.

Characteristic Piscean type. Is emotionally sensitive, compassionate, kindly, sympathetic, easy-going. Tend to be quickly moved to tears, and cannot bear to witness suffering – they either recoil, registering the suffering within themselves, or respond with the utmost help. Is the most unworldly of the 12 types. Very fluid nature, impossible to confine or conform to a disciplined or regimented pattern of behaviour, since it expresses the depth and hiddenness and variableness of the boundless ocean. Psychic, mediumistic.

Mentally very impressionable, receptive, intuitive, subtle with a creative imagination. Emotional, sensitive thoughts of the poet or priest rather than the scientist or soldier.

In love is intensely emotional, lovable, submissive, but likely to be confused and disillusioned by the cold realities of providing for a family.

Faults: impractical, over-emotional, too soft, careless, indecisive, touchy, secretive, incomprehensible, confused handling of affairs, gullible, extravagant, temperamental, dependent on others.

Ideal vocational activities: where will-power, rational thought are not essential factors. Where the intuitive, impressionable, sympathetic, imaginative and creative qualities can be exercised and developed. Tend to be musical, artistic, lyrical writers, poets, actors, psychics, the spinners of dreams. Desire to care for the sick, the needy, and animals. Attracted to the sea. As priests, sailors, social workers – especially in hospitals and institutions, chiropodists. To do with fluids, gases, anaesthetics, fish, plastics, footwear.

Psychologically the primitive urge to transcend the material, to break down all barriers, pierce through illusions of man-made social and religious structures of behaviour and conformity, have faith in the unknown. To enter into the feelings of others and share with others, but without that which binds and restricts to the personal. To experience simplicity of being.

Physiological: the feet. Reflex association with the abdomen and intestinal region (through Virgo). Tendency to feet troubles, and abdominal disorders often as a result of nervous and emotional stress, or weakness for alcohol. Drugs should be taken in moderation.

5

The geocentric framework

Earth: the starting-point in astrology. We live on Earth, and this must be our starting-point for determining the constantly changing angular positions of the Sun and planets relative to the Earth. These angular positions *as seen from the Earth* are the basis for astrological interpretation. These positions have to be measured, therefore the astronomers need a basic framework and points of reference to enable them to calculate the positions of the planets for any given moment of time, and for any place on Earth.

It is because for us the Earth is our standpoint that the Sun, Moon, planets, and even the distant constellations, *appear* to revolve about us. This is an illusion due to the rotation of the Earth on its axis. The positions of the planets, as given in the yearly Ephemerides used by astrologers, are the *geocentric* measurements, or the relative positions of the planets as viewed from the Earth (Gk.: *ge*, Earth). Measurements of the planets relative to the Sun as the central body of reference would be termed *heliocentric* (Gk.: *helios*, Sun).

First we must know what is a *great* circle, and what is a *small* circle, as referred to by astronomers, because the basic framework for measurements is composed of such circles. A *great* circle is any circle, the plane of which passes through the centre of the Earth. The equator is a great circle, since its plane passes through the centre of the Earth and is equidistant from the north and south poles. The equator corresponds to Latitude 0°. Now all other parallels of Latitude, which with meridians of Longitude are the coordinates for determining the exact location of any place on Earth, whether north or south of the equator are *small* circles. A small circle is any circle the plane of which does NOT pass through the centre of the Earth.

The *horizon, equator,* and *ecliptic* are the three main circles of reference for determining the positions of the planets as seen from any place on Earth. These three circles are *great* circles.

The Horizon, Prime Vertical, the Meridian. If you refer to Figure 6 the horizon is the great circle NESW (i.e., traced from N to E to S to W and back to N). These are known as the four Cardinal Points. This great circle is called the *rational* or *true* horizon. It is parallel to the *visible* or *apparent* horizon which is that customarily seen, the circular line formed by the apparent meeting of the earth and the sky, which is a *small* circle. The *celestial* or *sensible* horizon is the name given to the great circle of the rational horizon when it is produced to meet the heavens, i.e., extended beyond the sphere of the Earth to infinity.

The *zenith* is the point of the celestial sphere directly overhead for the observer, and is always at right-angles to the observer's horizon. The opposite point to the zenith is the *nadir*. We also speak of *secondaries* to the horizon, meaning great circles through the zenith and nadir, which are called *verticals*. The *Prime Vertical* is the vertical circle passing through the zenith, west point of horizon, nadir, and east point of horizon (see Figure 6). The Prime Vertical is, as its name implies, of prime importance as a circle of reference. In passing through the east and west points of the horizon its plane corresponds to the intersection of the horizon and the equator.

The Meridian is a great circle passing through the zenith and nadir (poles of the horizon), the poles of the equator, and the north and south points of the horizon. In Figure 6 it is the main circle in which are placed all the other circles. The horizon, equator, and Prime Vertical, which all pass through EW (Figure 6), are secondaries to the Meridian – because the poles of the Meridian are the east and west points of the horizon, being at right-angles to the Meridian. The importance of the Meridian is that the Sun crosses this at mid-day (for any place on Earth). The intersection of the ecliptic (Sun's apparent path) with the Meridian is what is known to astrologers as the *Midheaven*, or degree of culmination.

The Equator, First Point of Aries. A great circle, equidistant from the north and south poles, that marks the Earth's largest circumference, is called the *terrestrial equator*. Project the terrestrial equator to the celestial sphere and we call this 'extended' plane of the equator the *celestial equator*. It is called the *equinoctial*, because when the Sun crosses the equator (at the equinoxes) day and night are of equal length.

If you refer to Figure 7A you will see illustrated the Equatorial System

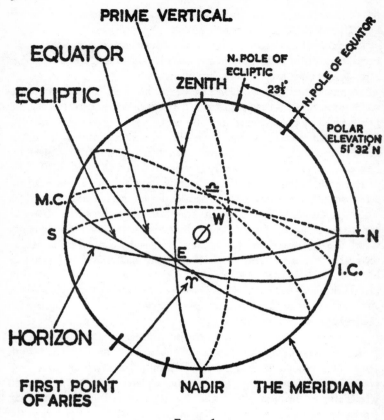

PRIME VERTICAL

EQUATOR

ECLIPTIC

N. POLE OF
ECLIPTIC

ZENITH   23½°   N. POLE OF EQUATOR

POLAR
ELEVATION
51° 32′ N

M.C.

S   W   N

E   I.C.

HORIZON

FIRST POINT   NADIR   THE MERIDIAN
OF ARIES

FIGURE 6
The Celestial Sphere
(Described for Polar Elevation 51° 32′ N, the latitude for London)

of celestial coordinates. Just as the Earth is belted by parallels of latitude and meridians of longitude for locating places on the terrestrial
sphere, so are the heavens belted to the astronomer with *parallels of
declination* and *meridians of right ascension*. The declination of a planet
corresponds exactly with terrestrial latitude. The equator is the natural
zero for declination, and planets on the equator are said to have a declination of 0°. Measurement is from the equator towards either of its
poles, according to whether a planet is north or south of the equator.
Declination must not be confused with *celestial latitude* which is the

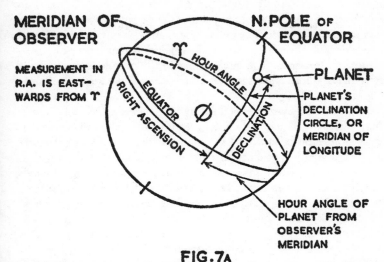

MERIDIAN OF OBSERVER

MEASUREMENT IN R.A. IS EAST-WARDS FROM ♈

N. POLE OF EQUATOR

PLANET

PLANET'S DECLINATION CIRCLE, OR MERIDIAN OF LONGITUDE

HOUR ANGLE OF PLANET FROM OBSERVER'S MERIDIAN

FIG. 7A
EQUATORIAL SYSTEM OF CELESTIAL CO-ORDINATES

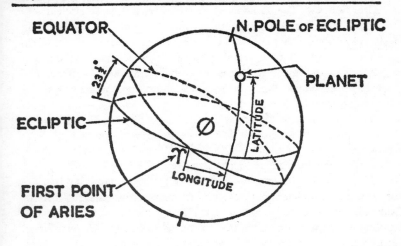

EQUATOR

N. POLE OF ECLIPTIC

PLANET

ECLIPTIC

FIRST POINT OF ARIES

FIG. 7B
ECLIPTIC SYSTEM OF CELESTIAL CO-ORDINATES

angular distance of a planet north or south of the ecliptic. There is no natural zero for either terrestrial longitude or right ascension, so an arbitrary choice is made. The great circle running through the poles and the position of Greenwich (England) is where measurement in terrestrial longitude begins. The intersections of the ecliptic and equator at the vernal equinox, called the *First Point of Aries*, is where measurement in right ascension begins.

The Equatorial System is defined by the *direction of the Earth's axis*. Thus, using the Equatorial System coordinates, a planet's position relative to the Earth is fixed by its distance in degrees, minutes and seconds of parallels of declination from the equator; and the distance measured *eastwards* of right ascension in degrees, minutes and seconds of arc, or in hours, minutes and seconds of time, from the First Point of Aries. The 360° of right ascension are divided, like the 360° of terrestrial longitude, into 24 hours. Hence, 1 hour in R.A. corresponds to 15° of arc; and 1° of arc to 4 minutes of time. However, the astrologer uses only one co-ordinate from the Equatorial System: *declination*. The corresponding measurement to right ascension is celestial longitude which will now be defined.

The Ecliptic, the Zodiac. The *ecliptic* is the great circle along which the Sun *appears* to travel in its journey around the Earth, taking one year to do so. Actually it is the great circle which the Earth traces around the Sun. But for astrological purposes we speak of the Sun 'going through the zodiacal signs' as it journeys along the ecliptic. The constellations whose names correspond to the signs of the zodiac are the 'background' to this path of the ecliptic, and we speak of the *zodiac* being a belt of the sky which has the ecliptic as its centre. This belt extends 8°–9° on either side of the ecliptic, within which the Sun, Moon, and major planets always remain. What this means in reality is that these major planets follow practically the same path or 'magnetic belt' as does the Earth in their orbits around the Sun. Pluto is rather the exception, its inclination to the ecliptic reaching as much as 17° (of latitude).

The Earth moves eastward as it rotates on its axis, and eastward in its ecliptical path, thus giving the impression that the Sun is moving westward among the stars. The point where the Sun's path along the ecliptic crosses the equator from south to north is called the *vernal equinox*. This occurs around 21st March. The second occasion in the same year when the Sun again crosses the equator, this time from north to south, is around 23rd September and is called the *autumnal equinox*.

The ecliptic cuts the equator at an angle of 23½°. This tells us that the pole of the ecliptic is about 23½° from the pole of the equator (Figure 6). When the Sun is at maximum declination 23½°N this marks the *summer solstice*, around 21st June; when the Sun's position in the ecliptic is 23½°S it is then the *winter solstice*, around 22nd December. Increase in declination is halted, the Sun, as it were, stands still, and declination then decreases. (Latin: *sistere*, to cause to stand still.)

The Ecliptic System (Figure 7B) is defined by the *plane of the Earth's orbit*, which fixes the position of the ecliptic. The co-ordinates of this system by which the position of a planet is determined, are *celestial longitude*, which is measured in degrees eastward from the First Point of Aries *to the meridian of longitude which passes through both the planet and the poles of the ecliptic*; and *celestial latitude*, which is measured north or south from the ecliptic in degrees (see Figure 7B). The First Point of Aries is a fixed point, and as celestial latitude and celestial longitude both refer to the ecliptic these measurements of a celestial body (planet) are unaffected by the diurnal motion (rotation of the Earth on its axis).

Astrologers rarely consider the latitude of a planet in their calculations. The co-ordinate used from the Ecliptic System is *celestial longitude*.

You cannot be expected to immediately grasp this essential astronomical structure. It will help you if you draw these diagrams of the relative positions of horizon, equator and ecliptic as you read about them. Try to bear in mind that the whole purpose of this framework is to enable us to know WHERE to locate a planet at any given time. We are not concerned with how far away the planet is. All we want to know is *at what angle as seen from the Earth a line from a planet strikes the Earth*. Declination, measured north or south from the *equator* to the planet, and celestial longitude measured *along the ecliptic* from the First Point of Aries to the planet, give us the required angular position.

Further reading

For a detailed description of the astronomical factors employed in astrology you are recommended to obtain *The Astrologer's Astronomical Handbook*, by Jeff Mayo (see Appendix I).

6

Time factors

The only data an astrologer requires from someone whose birth-chart he has to calculate are the *date*, *place*, and *time* of birth. For an accurate and distinctly individual chart-pattern this data must be EXACT: exact latitude and longitude of birth, exact time of birth. In the previous chapter you learned about the framework by which the angular relationship of any point on the Earth to any point (or planet) in the celestial sphere can be measured. Such measurement requires calculation. The calculation requires the fundamental points in *time and space* corresponding to an individual birth: the moment in time, the place of birth. The astrologer would then be able to calculate the exact position in celestial longitude and declination of each of the planets at the given moment of birth.

But to only know the positions of the planets without an 'Earth-framework' to refer them to, would give an incomplete picture astrologically. We call this 'Earth-framework' the 12 *mundane houses*, which you will learn about later. Right now we are concerned with the time-factors in calculating a chart.

Time. Time in reality is fictitious. It is a convenient form of measurement invented by man. Is it? The dynamic patterns of growth and evolution in all forms of Earth-life, or created by the apparent attraction and repulsion of gaseous and solid bodies hurtling in fantastic profusion and beauty through cosmic space, reveal to the scientist and the astronomer irrefutable rhythms and time-patterns – which in the case of the planets can be verified by the astronomer's ability to forecast exactly to the fraction of a degree in space where a certain planet will be for any given moment in the future.

What does this mean? Time, in terms of man's identifying moments or periods of observable growth, change, movement of a body from one point to another point in space, can correspond exactly to mathematical patterns or formulae. This is not just sheer coincidence. It is known that the interval between two successive transits of the same star over the same point on Earth is equal to 23 hours 56 minutes and 4.09 seconds of mean solar time. It is known that the gravitational attraction of the Sun and Moon on the Earth causes the axis of the Earth to tilt. Very slightly. A displacement of 50.26 seconds of celestial longitude in the time it takes the Earth to make one complete circuit of the Sun, one year. These great bodies of Earth, Moon and Sun interacting between their magnetic fields as they spin at colossal speeds towards inconceivable destinations, and yet these *regular* fractional displacements can be calculated to exact timetables. Space and time are indivisible. Matter and form, it would seem, are the equations of complex space-time energy-systems made manifest. Which prompts the thought: is all life, electron to star, ultimately to be understood in their individual forms and relationship to the Whole, through correspondence to a common time-scale? The basic space-time patterns from which these derive will, I am sure, be revealed to man's ever-searching, restless mind. But man's free-will to create his own patterns within the structure of his individual birth-pattern will always account for the margins of uncertainty in predicting cause and effect of phenomena. Quantum physics, dealing in terms of statistics and probabilities, admits margins of uncertainty, an indication that Nature does not quite produce an inexorable sequence of cause and effect.

However....

All measurements of time are really measurements in space; conversely, measurements in space depend on measurements of time. Remember this whilst you are learning the calculations of astrology, and what may at first appear as complex mathematics might be more clearly understood.

Tropical year, Sidereal year. Time, so far as we on Earth are concerned, exists because of, and therefore depends upon, the rotations of the Earth on its axis and its revolution about the Sun. This period of the Earth's revolution we call a *year*. It is a measurement between two successive vernal equinoxes, equal to 365 days 5 hours 48 minutes 46 seconds of mean solar time. We see it as the time the Sun takes to perform a complete revolution to the First Point of Aries. It is a natural, basic unit of time for man, who for thousands of years has recorded the recurrence of the seasons corresponding to this Earth-Sun cycle. This cycle is usually called the *tropical year* (Gk.: *trope*, turning) or the year of the seasons.

There is another kind of year. The *sidereal year* (Latin: *sidus*, star) which refers to the period of a complete (apparent) revolution by the Sun, measured from its passage across a secondary to the ecliptic through some fixed star until its return to that same star. This equals 365 days 6 hours 9 minutes 9.5 seconds. The sidereal year exceeds the tropical year by just over 20 minutes, and this difference, expressed in degrees of celestial longitude, gives us the figure of 50.26 seconds which I have mentioned as being the annual displacement resulting in the Precession of the Equinoctial Point.

Synodic month, sidereal month, calendar month. We have seen that the year, as a basic unit of time, refers to the Earth-Sun cycle. The next basic unit of time refers to the Earth-Moon cycle: the month. This name derives from the Moon.

The *synodic month* is the period between consecutive conjunctions of the Sun-Moon as seen from the Earth, thus it combines, in fact, the Earth-Sun-Moon cycle. The more commonly used name for this period is *lunation*. These points of conjunction are called New Moons, when the Sun and Moon have the same longitude. When they also have the same declination (i.e., the Moon is exactly on the ecliptic and between the Earth and the Sun) there is a solar eclipse. These conjunctions are of great importance in astrology. The mean or average synodic month is 29 days 12 hours 44 minutes 2.7 seconds.

The *sidereal month* is the Moon's period of revolution relative to the stars. The mean length of this period is 27 days 7 hours 43 minutes 11.5 seconds. This is the average time the Moon takes from one star back to the same star as seen from the Earth.

The *calendar month* is of course the month we use in our calendar, January, February, and so on.

The next unit of time is the *week*, which with its seven days comes to us from ancient Babylonia; even the names of the days can be traced back to the planetary gods. The length of the week corresponds roughly to one of the four phases of the Sun-Moon cycle or lunation.

Sidereal day, sidereal time. The fourth basic unit of time is the *day*. This is the period of the Earth's rotation on its axis. It may be measured with respect to the stars (sidereal day), the true Sun (apparent solar day), or the mean Sun (mean solar day).

Sidereal day is the true period of the Earth's rotation; the interval between two successive transits of a fixed star over the meridian of any place. In actual practice the First Point of Aries is used to define the sidereal day, and the instant this Point crosses the meridian, corresponding to 0h. 0m. 0s. *sidereal time*, the sidereal day begins. Although the hours are reckoned from 0–24 hours these do not quite correspond to the length of 24 mean solar hours. The sidereal day in mean solar units = 23 hours 56 minutes 4.09 seconds. Thus, each successive day the stars rise and set about 3m. 56s. earlier due to this difference between sidereal and mean solar days.

The sidereal day gives us *sidereal time*, which is the *hour angle* of the First Point of Aries when expressed in time. Now the hour angle can begin from the observer's meridian. If you refer to Figure 7A you will see a planet marked, with its meridian of longitude (sometimes called declination ˙circle) passing through it from the north pole of the equator to the equator. The hour angle of the planet is indicated with an arrow, and this angle is the interval of sidereal time that has elapsed since the planet was on the observer's meridian. Hour angle and sidereal time are measured in the *opposite* direction to right ascension; that is, *westwards* along the equator in hours, minutes and seconds up to 24 hours.

Local sidereal time, Greenwich Mean Time. When you come to use the *Ephemeris* for the example chart in this book you will find the *local sidereal time* given for noon at Greenwich for each day. At *any moment* the sidereal time is different for two different meridians, and this is why it is called *local* sidereal time when referred to a particular meridian. In *Raphael's Ephemerides*, most commonly used by astrologers, the local sidereal time is given for Greenwich each day because Greenwich local time (universally called *Greenwich Mean Time* (G.M.T.), or *Universal Time* (U.T.)) was legally defined to be the mean time to which clocks throughout the world are now synchronised. Greenwich was chosen because its meridian is internationally regarded as the standard meridian for the Earth.

If you turn to page 85, on which is reproduced a page from the *1942 Raphael's Ephemeris*, and look at the 3rd day of the month (July), in the third column under the heading *Sidereal Time* you will read 6.43.31. This is a similar reading of hour angle, in hours, minutes and seconds of sidereal time, *from* Greenwich meridian to another point westwards as mentioned two paragraphs back. Instead of this being a planet's hour angle it is the hour angle of the First Point of Aries. What it means, is that at noon (Greenwich Mean Time) on the 3rd July 1942, the hour angle measured westwards to the First Point of Aries (intersection of ecliptic-equator) *from* the Greenwich meridian was 6h. 43m. 31s. of sidereal time. This is called the local sidereal time for Green-

wich. On that day in July 1942, at noon G.M.T., the sidereal time of
6h. 43m. 31s. was unique for the Greenwich meridian (which is 0°). Any
other meridian from 0° westwards to 180°, or from 0° eastwards to
180°, would at that instant correspond to different sidereal times rang-
ing over the whole 24 sidereal hours.

For the following day, 4th July 1942, at noon G.M.T., you will note
there is now a different sidereal time, 6h. 47m. 28s. It has increased by
3m. 57s. Does this figure 'ring a bell' with you? Of course! – it is the
difference between sidereal day and mean solar day. What it means in
effect is, during the 24 hours (mean solar time) from noon 3rd July to
noon 4th July the Earth has rotated on its axis approximately 24h. 3m.
57s. of sidereal time with reference to the Greenwich meridian and the
First Point of Aries. Because for noon on these two consecutive days
the local sidereal time only varies by 3m. 57s. does not mean that the
Greenwich meridian moved no further from the First Point of Aries
than 3m. 57s. The Earth continued rotating! And the reading of sidereal
time for the Greenwich meridian changed with every moment of time,
from 6 hours to 7 hours and so on until about 17 hours later the meridian of Greenwich coincided with the First Point of Aries, when the
local sidereal time would read 0h. 0m. 0s. But the Earth continued
rotating, until by noon 4th July local sidereal time Greenwich read
6h. 47m. 28s. 24 hours of mean solar time had elapsed between the two
noons, but in the same period the Earth had rotated the full 24 hours
+ 3m. 57s. in sidereal time reckoning.

Apparent Solar Time, Mean Solar Time. When it is noon for
any place on Earth the Sun is at that moment crossing or transiting the
upper meridian of that place. The Sun transits a meridian twice in 24
hours. At midnight it transits the *lower meridian*. As our day begins
at midnight the *apparent solar day* is the interval between two successive
passages of the Sun across the *lower* meridian. This refers to the passage
of the *true* Sun, which is the actual Sun in the heavens, and its measurement is called *apparent solar time*. Now because the orbit of the Earth
about the Sun does not describe a circle, but is an ellipse, oval-shaped,
this causes the Earth to move round the Sun with variable speed. The
closer to the Sun (perihelion) the faster it goes; the further from the
Sun (aphelion) the more its speed decreases. So, the *apparent* speed of
the Sun as seen from the Earth against the background of stars varies
similarly. Around 23rd December the solar day from solar noon to
solar noon is 51 seconds longer than it is around 23rd September. Obviously there would be no sense in making clocks which kept pace with

these variations in the apparent speed of the true Sun. Thus, a fictitious Sun was invented and was called the *mean* Sun. It is a *point* which moves round the ecliptic and is never very far in hour angle from the true Sun, but it moves *uniformly*, which the true Sun does not. Its rate of motion is the average, throughout the year, of the true Sun's angular motion in the ecliptic, and this is known as *mean solar time*. The addition or subtraction to be made daily to convert apparent solar time into mean solar time is called the *Equation of Time*. The Equation of Time is nil on only 4 occasions in the year, when the speed of the true Sun is identical to that of the mean Sun: on or about 16th April, 14th June, 1st September and 25th December.

Local time, zone time, standard time. From what has been said you will understand that for a given place and a given instant the *apparent local solar time* is the interval since the Sun crossed the meridian of that place – dependent on whether this time is counted from the lower or the upper meridian. For astronomical purposes time is counted from midnight, when the Sun transits the lower meridian. If, in a country, the day is divided into two 12-hour periods, a.m. and p.m., then the Sun's transit of both lower and upper meridians are considered. E.g., if it were 5 hours and 20 minutes since the Sun crossed the upper meridian of Bristol, England, the *apparent local solar time* would be 5.20 p.m., but for the astronomer, counting the time from the Sun's transit of the lower meridian, it would be 17h. 20m. (12h. − 5h. 20m.). This, however, would not correspond exactly to *local mean solar time*, which would for England as a whole be *Greenwich Mean Time*, but would differ according to the Equation of Time for that day.

For very large countries or expanses of ocean a system of *zones* is used to fix the time for chosen ranges of longitude. This is because with the rotation of the Earth the Sun appears to take roughly 1 hour to pass over any 15° of terrestrial longitude (360° of the Earth sphere divided by 24 hours = 15°). Or 4 minutes of apparent solar time to pass between each degree of longitude. Now think of the absurdity of a vast country like the United States using the same local mean solar time as would apply to New York. For instance, San Francisco is $48\frac{1}{2}°$ of longitude further west than New York. If the whole of the U.S.A. used New York local time, when the Sun crossed the San Francisco meridian at mid-day the local clocks would instead be showing the time to be 3.14 p.m. ($48\frac{1}{2}° \times 4$ minutes = 3h. 14 m.). It would be equally impractical for each locality to set their clocks to apparent local solar time.

Most countries have now adopted Standard Time based on Greenwich Mean Time. *Zone Time* is used at sea, *Standard Time* on land. It is equal to local civil time at adopted central meridians. These meridians are usually 15° apart, and central in the time zones. Time changes abruptly between neighbouring zones, and on opposite sides of the 180° meridian time changes by a whole day. All clocks in a particular time zone are synchronised. The variations in time between zones are in multiples of 1 hour or ½ hour. Therefore when it is noon at Greenwich (G.M.T.) in New York (74°W longitude) it will be 7 a.m., because New York is in a time zone 5 hours slow on Greenwich. San Francisco is in a different time zone to New York and it will be 4 a.m. there when it is noon at Greenwich. *Note: see Time references*, Appendix I.

Summer Time. It has become customary in many countries to advance the clocks 1 hour during several months around the summer period of the year. As we all know, this is called *Summer Time* or *Daylight Saving Time*. In 1916 this was introduced into Great Britain and has been used ever since. During the War years *Double Summer Time* was used during summer and the extra hour of usual Summer Time applied for the rest of the year. A complete summary of these times are listed in Appendix III. Unfortunately, it is difficult to obtain an exact and comprehensive list of *all* periods of Daylight Saving Time for *all* countries but the fullest lists obtainable for both *Daylight Saving* and *Standard Times* are in the *Time Changes* books (see Appendix I).

Ephemeris time. *Raphael's Ephemeris* was based on G.M.T. until 1959. Since 1960 it has been calculated in *Ephemeris Time* (E.T.). It is the theoretical uniform time system employed in gravitation theories of the Sun, Moon and planets, used side by side with Universal Time, especially for making predictions. E.T. was identical with G.M.T. early in 1903, but the two have slowly diverged, and E.T. is now (1962) 35 seconds in advance of G.M.T. This is of no practical consequence; however accurately an astrologer likes to interpret a chart a discrepancy of 35 seconds won't matter! However, for correctness 1 minute should be subtracted from all times given in E.T. to convert these to G.M.T.

Essential time-factors. The student of astrology should make an effort to understand the different time-systems mentioned. It is not necessary to remember exact details or figures, but a sound grasp of the purpose of these time-systems, and from which astronomical factors they arise, will make for a clearer understanding of astrological theory.

In the previous chapter you learned that the three *most important points of reference* for determining the exact angular relationship between the planetary bodies for any given time are:

> The First Point of Aries
> The East Point of the Horizon
> The Midheaven, or Upper Meridian.

The *most important time-factors* to learn how to apply in the calculation of a birth-chart are:

> Sidereal Time
> Greenwich Mean Time
> Zone or Standard Time.

Given the birth-data (date, time, place of birth) the local sidereal time can be accurately calculated, as you will learn presently. This represents the angle, measured in time, linking the First Point of Aries with the meridian of birthplace. With this known factor combined with the terrestrial latitude of birthplace, the East Point of the Horizon is included in the formula. From which can be determined the two vital *angles* in the birth-chart: Ascendant-Descendant polarity, and the Midheaven (M.C.)-Imum Coeli (I.C.) polarity.

Recommended reading

Time factors: *The Astrologer's Astronomical Handbook*, by Jeff Mayo (see Appendix I).

7

Ascendant and Midheaven: the angles

You have learned that the planets represent life-principles in man, which function through any of 12 basic types or modes of expression (signs). Each life-principle and each of the 12 basic types are contained within you and me, as essential energy and substance of being, but as individuals we each respond more readily to certain of these factors than we do to others. The predominant factors are responsible for distinguishing characteristics and behaviour. Later you will learn how to assess the predominant factors.

Two very important factors which are *always* predominant in an individual's personal make-up are the Ascendant and the Midheaven (the latter usually called M.C., from Latin: *Medium Coeli*). These refer to what are called the *angles* (see Figure 1). They can only be calculated when the time (or approximate time) of birth is known. In Chapter 9 you will learn how to calculate these. At present I will introduce you briefly to their derivation and their functions in the general psychological structure of any one of us.

The Ascendant is determined by the degree of the ecliptic which is rising (due to the rotation of the Earth on its axis) on the eastern horizon at birth, that is, at a given moment of time, viewed at a horizontal angle from the birthplace. You must get it clear that the Ascendant is only a fixed point *in the birth-chart*. In reality, because the Earth is continually rotating, there is a new degree of the ecliptic rising over the horizon every moment of the day and night. This Rising Degree, as it is called, is always the degree on the cusp (division between adjoining houses) of the 1st house of the birth-chart.

The Ascendant is more than just this single degree. It is the whole zodiacal sign containing the Rising Degree. We call its opposite sign, containing the degree which at the same moment is *descending* below the *western* horizon, the *Descendant*. This is always the degree on the cusp of the 7th house. For instance, if the Ascendant were Leo 5°, the Descendant would be Aquarius 5°.

The Midheaven refers to that degree where the ecliptic reaches its highest point (in its ascent above the horizon) at the meridian of any place at a given time (see Figure 6). This degree is also called the *culminating* degree.

We call the degree which is opposite to the degree of the Midheaven which at the same moment is the *lowest* point of the ecliptic below the horizon and intersecting the meridian of the birthplace, the I.C. (Latin: *Imum Coeli*). If Taurus 7° were on the M.C., Scorpio 7° would be on the I.C. Refer also to the M.C. and I.C. in Figure 1.

The Descendant and I.C. in the psychological sense are of considerably less importance to the Ascendant and M.C. However, they have a distinct value in regard to the house (sphere of life) they correspond to in the chart, and also indicate complementary characteristics to those associated with the particular Ascendant and M.C. signs. For example, a person with an Aries Ascendant will have a typically assertive, me-first, impulsive personality; but will need to balance these powerful traits by exercising the more cooperative and less fiery attributes of its polarity, Libra, on the Descendant.

We get a clue to the astrologer's interpretation of the Ascendant when we remember that the Sun *rises* every morning on the eastern horizon, and *sets* each evening on the western horizon – wherever you view this phenomenon from on Earth. Of course, the Sun is not going to be actually on the eastern horizon at the birth moment of each one of us, simply because the Ascendant refers to the degree rising on the eastern horizon. The Sun will only be close to the Ascendant in the charts of those born around sunrise; as it will always be close to the M.C. in the charts of those born around noon; and close to the Descendant in the charts of those born around sunset; and close to the I.C. in the charts of those born around midnight.

The Ascendant has a significant relationship to *awakening* self-consciousness in man, hence the *personality*. We see the analogy here, the eastern horizon representing dawn, the darkness of night (as the unconscious) broken by the first light of a new day.

The M.C. has a significant relationship to *established* self-consciousness, hence the *Ego*. At noon the influence of the Sun is most powerful, the light of day is brightest, analogous to consciousness at its most 'wide awake'.

The Ascendant, therefore, corresponds to that aspect of man we call the *personality*. Jung speaks of the *Persona*, from the Greek *persona*, meaning a mask, a pretended character, worn by an actor. Because the Ascendant derives from the horizon of a person's birthplace, and is determined by the Earth's rotation, an interesting yet nevertheless consistent fact becomes clear: the personality or Persona is an adopted attitude largely conditioned and impressed upon an individual by his particular Earth-environment. According to which zodiacal type represents the Ascendant so will that individual draw on its characteristics with which to mould this mask, this pose, between his real nature and the outside world of his environment. The Persona is one's form of adjustment and immediate response to the world-outside-oneself. It can be the face a man wears whilst he projects himself into his business and social activities, concealing much of his true character that only his intimates – and often not even they – know exists. The Ascendant, however, does not supply the complete picture of the Persona, but the essential part of it. We must also realise that the Persona is not entirely some sort of mask or false nature we hide behind. True, the more sophisticated we become the more powerfully the Persona shuts off our natural self. But it is also through the mode of the Ascendant or Persona that we will learn to differentiate between what we find within our true self and what we recognise in others.

When assessing the personality or Persona, therefore, you must look primarily to the Ascendant for the strength and mode of one's conscious adjustment to environment, according to the sign on the Ascendant. The Ascendant is like the lens of a camera: all other factors in the chart have to be 'focused through' the Ascendant, and so become modified by its attitude.

The definition of the *Ego* varies with different writers. I prefer Jung's suggestion that it is essentially the focal point of consciousness. The conscious aspect of ourselves might be compared to the visible part of an island jutting from the sea; all that is the island below the sea is our unconscious; the sea itself is the collective unconscious we share with all mankind. The visible island is the Ego, that part of ourselves which identifies ourselves as a separate being.

Jupiter and Saturn in a chart indicate the ability to express oneself consciously, and therefore are important significators of the quality and growth of the Ego. The essential focal point of the Ego, however, for its objective function of consciously relating oneself to exterior reality, or of consciously experiencing oneself, is through the zodiacal type or sign at the M.C.

For interpreting the sign on the Ascendant or M.C. in their special functions as Persona and Ego, refer to Chapter 4 for characteristics associated with the signs.

8

The houses: spheres of life

You have learned that a basic stipulation of astrology if one is to interpret the nature of anything is to know *the moment when it began* and its
angular relationship on Earth, at that moment, to the whole cosmic pattern. We need to know how to measure and fix its beginning in time
and space. It is because of the construction of a basic framework
for fixing the cosmic pattern existing at any moment that the
interpretative value of astrology can be tested by anyone who has
the patience and intelligence to learn how to use its relatively simple
formulae.

There are 12 houses, referred to by their numbers. If you refer to
Figure 8 you will see the order in which the numbered houses are
arranged round the chart. This is always the same, the 1st house starting
from the degree on the Ascendant. It is only the placing of the signs and
the planets in these houses that varies with individual charts. Therefore
you can buy 'blank' chart-forms, with the houses already numbered,
ready for you to enter the signs and planets.

Correspondence between houses, signs and planets. You will
observe in Figure 8 signs and planets entered against the houses. This is
to show you the *basic correspondence* between matters connected with a
house and the nature of a particular sign, called the *natural* sign of the
house. Since the principle of each planet has a definite association with
a certain sign (or two signs) there is also a recognisable affinity between
planets and houses, although in actual interpretation you do not need
to complicate things by taking these basic correspondences into consideration until the reading of a chart is second nature to you.

For instance, the 1st house is associated with matters arising from a
distinctly *personal* attitude to life; the 1st sign, Aries, represents the
me-first, self-centred attitude; Mars (associated with Aries) represents the
life-principle of activity through *self-assertion* and energetic expression.

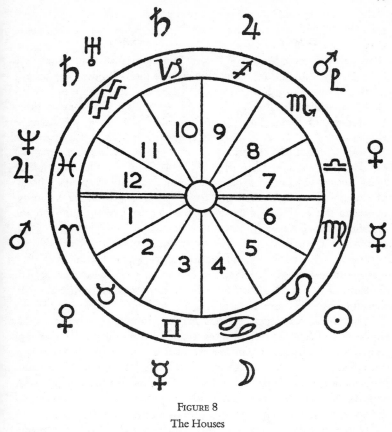

FIGURE 8
The Houses

It will be a useful exercise for you to go through all the houses, signs and planets in this way.

Systems of house-division. The dividing points between the houses are known as *cusps*. There are numerous systems of house-division favoured by different astrologers, dividing the equator, the ecliptic, or the Prime Vertical into 12 parts. One system, the Placidean, still commonly used though proven worthless, particularly since it presents a gross distortion and misrepresentation of individuals born in the higher latitudes (beyond 60°), divides *time*, taken to cover space, into 12 parts. The system of Equal House Division taught in this book, which I personally use, is the oldest of all systems (except that in its earliest use the M.C. was not incorporated). Students must always judge the different systems for themselves, which they can learn about from other astrological books.

Equal house system. The Rising Degree or Ascendant is taken as the starting-point and represents the cusp of the 1st house. The ecliptic is divided into 12 *equal* sections (called *lunes*) of 30°. Therefore, whatever degree is on the Ascendant or 1st house cusp is also on every other house cusp. Only the signs on the cusps vary. Look at the example chart (Figure 1). 4° 52' Pisces corresponds to the 1st house cusp. The 1st house extends 30°, or exactly the number of degrees to a sign, so if we count forward 30° this brings us to 4° 52' Aries which is the 2nd house cusp. 4° 52' Taurus is the 3rd house cusp, and so on, each house of equal length just as the signs are of equal length. Since we know these are the same we only write the degrees and minutes on the Ascendant, not every cusp.

In what are called the *Quadrant* House Systems the M.C. always corresponds to the 10th house cusp. Using Equal House only very rarely (when the M.C. is exactly 90° from the Ascendant) does it correspond to the 10th cusp. The M.C. can appear in either the 8th, 9th, 10th or 11th houses, according to the time of the year and the time of the day for which the chart is cast. This is because of the variation in time taken for certain signs to ascend over the eastern horizon. In every 24 hours all 12 signs ascend over the eastern horizon (in latitudes below the Arctic Circle), and each degree of each sign culminates in the south at the upper meridian (M.C.), goes the full circle until it appears on the eastern horizon again next day. This is due to the rotation of the Earth on its axis. In northern latitudes the signs Cancer to Sagittarius are termed signs of *long ascension*, because they take a long time to ascend; the signs Capricorn to Gemini are termed signs of *short ascension*, because they take less time to ascend. The opposite occurs in southern latitudes. Thus, when a sign of long ascension is on the Ascendant the number of degrees between it and the M.C. will account for the latter appearing in the 8th or 9th house; whereas fewer degrees will separate the Ascendant and M.C. when a sign of short ascension is rising, and the M.C. will appear in either the 10th or 11th house. Near the equator there is not this variance between the signs.

Spheres of Life Activities. Traditionally the houses are called *mundane* houses because they refer to everyday life-on-Earth activities. The planets and signs represent the psychological make-up, and according to which houses these are associated with in an individual chart so can we see those aspects of life-activities and interests these energies and impulses of the nature will tend to be most focused on.

As with the first six signs applying, in a broad sense, more to the desires or acquisitions of the person for himself, and the last six to the desire to enter more into experience with other people, so does this tendency apply to the houses.

Keyword formula for interpreting the houses. A planet and sign 'placed in' a house means that the life-principle (planet) will function in a typical way (sign) and this energy be focused particularly on activities and matters connected with that house.

1st house: self-centred interests.
2nd house: possessions and personal security.
3rd house: relationship of self to environment.
4th house: self, possessions, and intimate relatives as a basis for new growth.
5th house: re-creation and exposition of self.
6th house: conformity and service to the community, conditioned by health and efficiency.
7th house: identification and unity of self with others at personal level.
8th house: self-sacrifice, and shared resources with others.
9th house: projection of self to new horizons.
10th house: social status, in terms of material responsibilities and necessity.
11th house: identification of self with group-objectives.
12th house: self-abnegation in service, or self-disintegration, escapism, confinement.

House meanings

1st house. Keywords: *self-centred interests.*

Of particular importance because the Ascending sign dominates this house, hence its being the sphere of self-centred interests.

Its sphere of life has a correspondence with the principle of *Mars*, and the objective and impulsive attitude of *Aries*.

Hence, *relates to activities and matters* which are one's own special interest, and through which one seeks to determine separateness of being and personality. Also has a significant bearing on physical characteristics and tendencies to particular illness.

2nd house. Keywords: *possessions and personal security.*

Its sphere of life has a correspondence with the principle of *Venus,* and the productive and possessive attitude of *Taurus.*

Hence, *relates to activities and matters* connected with one's need for material possessions and the accumulation of money, representative of oneself, one's uniqueness, power, resourcefulness; and the instinctive need for personal security, comfort and contentment.

3rd house. Keywords: *relationship of self to environment.*

Its sphere of life has a correspondence with the principle of *Mercury,* and the adaptive and communicative attitude of *Gemini.*

Hence, *relates to activities and matters* connected with one's need to relate and adjust oneself to the immediate environment created by circumstances, involving near relatives such as brothers and sisters, and casual acquaintances, neighbours. Activities will be of a close communicative nature, short journeys, direct mental contact. The mental quality and activity shown will refer to the normal expressiveness required for daily conversation and letter-writing, and not deep thought or study (9th house).

4th house. Keywords: *self, possessions, and intimate relatives as a basis for new growth.*

Its sphere of life has a correspondence with the principle of the *Moon,* and the protective and defensive attitude of *Cancer.*

Hence, *relates to activities and matters* connected with one's need to make a home or base or any place within which to contain and protect that which is and belongs to oneself. Thus, essentially connected with one's family, parental influence, property owned or rented.

5th house. Keywords: *re-creation and exposition of self.*

Its sphere of life has a correspondence with the principle of the *Sun,* and the creative and impressive attitude of *Leo.*

Hence, *relates to activities and matters* connected with one's need for expressions of creativeness, happiness; display of one's power and prowess. Thus, games, sports, pleasures, creative art, and risky ventures such as gambling, speculation, love-making. The organising of talents and qualities into an impressive and powerful projection of one's own image. Also the offspring of one's mind (ideas) as well as of the body.

6th house. Keywords: *conformity and service to the community, conditioned by health and efficiency.*

Its sphere of life has a correspondence with the principle of *Mercury*, and the critical and analytical attitude of *Virgo*.

Hence, *relates to activities and matters* connected with one's need to function within and serve the community as a necessary and inter-dependent part of the whole; equally the service given to oneself by others. The ability to formulate and adhere to a disciplined pattern of 'wholesomeness' for one's personal life, so that one can function effectively and wholly; which in effect implies inevitable conformity to the 'pattern of the community' – for man lives upon man. Efficiency and wholesomeness depend upon one's health, and this house gives important indications of possible sickness.

7th house. Keywords: *identification and unity of self with others at personal level.*

Its sphere of life has a correspondence with the principle of *Venus*, and the urge for relationship and harmony of *Libra*.

Hence, *relates to activities and matters* connected with one's need to identify and unite oneself on equal terms with others. This could be through partnership, particularly marriage. Suggests possible type of the opposite sex one is attracted to, through whom the self seeks balance and wholeness.

As the 1st house focuses on *oneself*, the 7th focuses interest on *other people*.

8th house. Keywords: *self-sacrifice, and shared resources with others.*

Its sphere of life has a correspondence with the principles of *Pluto* and *Mars*, and the intense and penetrating attitude of *Scorpio*.

Hence, *relates to activities and matters* connected with one's need to share one's resources and possessions with, or measure of material dependence on, others; possible benefits through bequests, legacies. Nature or possibility of self-sacrifice, regeneration (true spiritual conversion – not to any orthodox faith). Possible nature of one's death.

As the 2nd house focuses on *one's own* possessions and resources, the 8th focuses on the need to share these with *others*.

9th house. Keywords: *projection of self to new horizons.*

Its sphere of life has a correspondence with the principle of *Jupiter*, and the broad and extensive attitude of *Sagittarius*.

Hence, *relates to activities and matters* connected with one's need to experience life beyond the limited horizons of commonplace existence. This can be through foreign travel or communication; deep and extensive mental studies. Traditionally this includes philosophy, the law, religion, higher education, publishing and dream experiences. Also relatives, such as in-laws, who are not of one's blood-stock.

As the 3rd house focuses on one's *immediate* environment and *close* communication, the 9th house focuses interest on *distant* horizons, *longer* communications.

10th house. Keywords: *social status, in terms of material responsibility and necessity.*

Its sphere of life has a correspondence with the principle of *Saturn* and the responsible and disciplined attitude of *Capricorn.*

Hence, *relates to activities and matters* connected with one's need and capacity to establish oneself successfully and usefully in the community. One's career.

As the 4th house focuses on one's *home* and *family* interests, the 10th house focuses on one's expression and interests-*outside the home.*

11th house. Keywords: *identification of self with group-objectives.*

Its sphere of life has a correspondence with the principles of *Uranus* and *Saturn*, and the detached and humanistic attitude of *Aquarius.*

Hence, *relates to activities and matters* connected with one's need to achieve objectives for the benefit of a group or community, as distinct from personal aims and ambitions. Friendships, without need for personal ties. Reformative and unconventional activities. Interests in clubs and societies. Traditionally one's 'hopes and wishes'.

As the 5th house focuses on *personal* creative interests, the 11th house focuses on *communal* creative interests.

12th house. Keywords: *self-abnegation in service, or self-disintegration, escapism, confinement.*

Its sphere of life has a correspondence with the principles of *Neptune* and *Jupiter*, and the impressionable and nebulous attitude of *Pisces.*

Hence, *relates to activities and matters* connected with one's need to experience life wholly, freed from restrictions, social barriers, personal limitations; or the likelihood of confinement, social isolation, development of patterns of escape and withdrawal from realities. Association with hospitals, mental institutes, prisons, convent or monastic life, secret activities. Selfless deeds unconsciously prompted by conscience as amends for past wrongs.

As the 6th house focuses on *health* and *services* indicative of personal efficiency, the 12th house focuses on *chronic ill-health* and more *profound service* for mankind.

9

Calculating the natal chart

From my experience as tutor to beginners in astrology I know that the majority face their first attempts at calculation with a totally unnecessary sense of awe. No doubt you may be feeling the same, particularly if, after only one reading the chapters on the astronomical and time factors appeared confusing and completely 'foreign' to anything you have read before. With further reading, and once you have employed these measurements in time and space in calculating a birth-chart, these factors will be more closely seen as a sequence of simple and logical steps for the purpose of relating the planets to a specified place on Earth.

Presently we are going to calculate an example chart. When you have done this you will know how to set up a chart for a birth anywhere on Earth, and to any time-system. Whilst you are learning to understand the procedure through the example chart in this book you will not need to spend a single penny on reference books or other items. All data appertaining to the example chart are contained in this book. But before you can calculate further charts for births other than July 1942 you will need to buy an *ephemeris* for the year in question and the following books listed under *The Tools Needed for Calculation*. Details about these will be found in Appendix I.

The tools needed for calculation

(a) A blank birth-chart form (sheet of paper until you buy these), scribbling-pad and pall-pen;

(b) *Ephemeris* for year of birth;

(c) *Tables of Houses*;

(d) *Pluto Ephemeris* or *Tables*;

(e) *Gazetteer* for finding latitude and longitude of birthplace;

(f) Lists or books giving Daylight Saving and Standard Times;

(g) Table for Converting Degrees and Minutes of Longitude into Longitude Equivalent in Time (see Appendix V).

The Ephemeris. This is a booklet published annually, containing the positions of the Sun, Moon and planets at noon Greenwich Mean Time for every day of the year. Some publications give positions at midnight. In my experience the most reliable and comprehensive data is found in *Raphael's Ephemerides*, which have been published since about 1820. The planets' positions given enable one to calculate their celestial longitude and declination corresponding to any second in time for the year in question, as viewed from any place on Earth.

Tables of houses. A booklet containing tables to which one refers for finding the sign and degree on the Ascendant and M.C. corresponding to the local sidereal time at birth, for latitude of birthplace. Actually all the house cusps are calculated, but for the Placidean System of House Division. However, the Ascendant and M.C. which are the same for the Equal House System are all we need to extract from these tables. These are based on the original calculations of the first 'Raphael', R. C. Smith, in 1821, and have been practically the only tables available, hence the 'blind acceptance' of the Placidean System by students, which, as I've already stated, cannot be of any value since the houses become ridiculously distorted in the higher latitudes. If a system cannot be applied to the whole sphere of the Earth, wherever birth occurs, it is worthless.

Pluto Ephemeris. This gives the positions of the planet Pluto for the years prior to 1933. Since 1934 Pluto's positions appear in *Raphael's Ephemerides*.

The birth-data. The key to a chart: the *time*, *date* and *place* of birth. The more accurate the known birth-time, the more accurately will the indications in the chart apply to the individual concerned. When the time is not known a so-called 'flat' chart can be set up, by placing Aries 0° on the cusp of the 1st house and inserting the planets to their noon positions as given in the *Ephemeris* for the birthday. Houses are ignored. Or a speculative time of birth may be assessed by what is called *rectification* (see Chapter 15).

The four stages in calculation

1. Determining the time of birth in *Greenwich Mean Time*.
2. Finding the *local sidereal time* at birth.

3. Calculating the *planets' positions*.
4. Calculating and tabulating the *planetary aspects*.

Stage I: determining the time of birth in Greenwich Mean Time

Why in Greenwich Mean Time (G.M.T.)? For no other reason than that the *Ephemeris* is based on G.M.T. Therefore, if the time of birth is given in any category of time other than G.M.T. this has to be converted into G.M.T. This will be self-explanatory with a couple of examples, and if you re-read Chapter 6.

There are 5 categories of time in which the birth-moment may be given to you:

1. In *G.M.T.* for births since 1880 in the British Isles.
2. In *Summer Time*. In this case subtract 1 hour to convert to G.M.T. Summer Time has been used in various countries besides the British Isles. A complete list of British Summer Times is given in Appendix III.
3. In *Double Summer Time*, used during the years 1941–45 and 1947 in the British Isles. Subtract 2 hours to convert to G.M.T.
4. In *Zone or Standard Time* of countries outside the British Isles. See Appendix IV. If birthplace is *east* of Greenwich, the Standard Time will be in *advance* of G.M.T., and the difference must be subtracted to convert to G.M.T. If *west* of Greenwich it will be *behind* or slow of G.M.T., and the difference must be added to convert to G.M.T.
5. In *Local Mean Time*. Used in the British Isles for births prior to 1880, and in rare instances elsewhere. Refer to a gazetteer for the longitude of birthplace. The difference in time between that of Greenwich and that of the birthplace is determined by their *difference in longitude*. Call the degrees of longitude minutes of time, and the minutes of longitude seconds of time, and *multiply them by* 4 (this is because the Sun travels the equivalent of 1° of longitude in 4 minutes of time). If the birthplace is *west* of Greenwich ADD the result to the given birth-time; if *east* SUBTRACT the result from the given time, to convert to G.M.T.

Now to begin working on our example chart (Figure 1).

It is for a birth at 0.34 a.m. British Double Summer Time, 4th July 1942, at Windsor, England.

Referring to our gazetteer we find Windsor has a latitude of 51° 28′N, and a longitude of 0° 36′W.

NEW MOON—July 13, 0h. 3m. 6s. p.m.

14					JULY, 1942.						[RAPHAEL'S
D M	Neptune.		Herschel.		Saturn.		Jupiter.		Mars.		
	Lat.	Dec.	Lat.	Dec.	Lat.	Dec.	Lat.	Dec.	Lat.	Declin.	
1	1 N 19	2 N 18	0 S 10	20 N 32	1 S 44	19 N 44	0 S 7	23 N 15	1 N 14	18 N 44	18 N 34
3	1 19	2 17	0 10	20 33	1 45	19 46	0 7	23 14	1 14	18 23	18 13
5	1 19	2 17	0 10	20 34	1 45	19 48	0 7	23 13	1 13	18 2	17 51
7	1 18	2 16	0 10	20 35	1 45	19 50	0 6	23 12	1 13	17 40	17 28
9	1 18	2 15	0 10	20 36	1 45	19 52	0 6	23 11	1 12	17 17	17 6
11	1 18	2 14	0 10	20 37	1 45	19 54	0 6	23 9	1 12	16 54	16 42
13	1 18	2 13	0 10	20 38	1 45	19 56	0 6	23 8	1 11	16 31	16 19
15	1 18	2 12	0 10	20 39	1 45	19 58	0 6	23 7	1 11	16 7	15 55
17	1 18	2 11	0 10	20 40	1 45	20 0	0 6	23 5	1 10	15 42	15 30
19	1 18	2 10	0 10	20 41	1 45	20 2	0 5	23 4	1 10	15 18	15 5
21	1 18	2 9	0 10	20 42	1 46	20 3	0 5	23 2	1 9	14 53	14 40
23	1 18	2 8	0 10	20 43	1 46	20 5	0 5	23 0	1 8	14 27	14 14
25	1 18	2 7	0 10	20 44	1 46	20 7	0 5	22 59	1 8	14 1	13 48
27	1 18	2 6	0 10	20 45	1 46	20 8	0 4	22 57	1 7	13 35	13 22
29	1 18	2 5	0 10	20 46	1 46	20 10	0 4	22 55	1 7	13 9	12 55
31	1 18	2 3	0 10	20 46	1 46	20 11	0 4	22 53	1 6	12 42	

D M	D W	Sidereal Time.	☉ Long.	☉ Dec.	☽ Long.	☽ Lat.	☽ Dec.	MIDNIGHT.	
								☽ Long.	☽ Dec.
		H. M. S.							
1	W	6 35 38	9♋ 0 25	23 N 8	20♒42	15 N 1	20 13 S 20	27♒47 59	11 S 35
2	Th	6 39 34	9 57 37	23 4	4✕46 34	0 9	41	11✕38 0	7 41
3	F	6 43 31	10 54 48	23 0	18 22 28	1 S 7	5 38	25 0 13	3 32
4	S	6 47 28	11 52 0	22 55	1♈31 39	2 14	1 26	7♈57 15	0 N 39
5	☉	6 51 24	12 49 12	22 50	14 17 31	3 12	2 N 41	20 33 1	4 41
6	M	6 55 21	13 46 25	22 44	26 47 17	3 59	6 36	2♉51 54	8 25
7	Tu	6 59 17	14 43 38	22 38	8♉56 25	4 34	10 9	14 58 20	11 45
8	W	7 3 14	15 40 51	22 31	20 58 10	4 57	13 13	26 56 22	14 33
9	Th	7 7 10	16 38 4	22 25	2Ⅱ53 23	5 7	15 44	8Ⅱ49 34	16 44
10	F	7 11 7	17 35 18	22 17	14 45 18	5 3	17 33	20 40 53	18 12
11	S	7 15 3	18 32 32	22 10	26 36 37	4 46	18 38	2♋32 43	18 52
12	☉	7 19 0	19 29 46	22 2	8♋29 27	4 17	18 54	14 27 1	18 43
13	M	7 22 57	20 27 1	21 53	20 25 36	3 36	18 19	26 25 25	17 44
14	Tu	7 26 53	21 24 16	21 45	2♌26 39	2 46	16 56	8♌29 31	15 56
15	W	7 30 50	22 21 31	21 35	14 34 14	1 47	14 45	20 41 2	13 24
16	Th	7 34 46	23 18 47	21 20	26 50 11	0 43	11 54	3♍ 1 58	10 15
17	F	7 38 43	24 16 3	21 16	9♍16 41	0 N 25	8 28	15 34 41	6 35
18	S	7 42 39	25 13 18	21 6	21 56 18	1 32	4 37	28 21 54	2 34
19	☉	7 46 36	26 10 35	20 55	4♎51 53	2 36	0 28	11♎26 34	1 S 40
20	M	7 50 32	27 7 51	20 44	18 6 18	3 34	3 S 48	24 51 22	5 55
21	Tu	7 54 29	28 5 8	20 33	1♏42 0	4 21	7 59	8♏38 19	9 58
22	W	7 58 26	29 2 24	20 21	15 40 22	4 55	11 50	22 48 3	13 33
23	Th	8 2 22	29 59 41	20 9	0♐ 1 6	5 11	15 6	7♐19 7	16 25
24	F	8 6 19	0♌56 59	19 57	14 41 30	5 7	17 29	22 7 30	18 16
25	S	8 10 15	1 54 17	19 44	29 36 15	4 43	18 44	7♑ 6 42	18 52
26	☉	8 14 12	2 51 35	19 31	14♑37 46	3 59	18 41	22 8 18	18 9
27	M	8 18 8	3 48 54	19 18	29 37 8	2 59	17 19	7♒ 3 11	16 11
28	Tu	8 22 5	4 46 13	19 5	14♒25 27	1 47	14 48	21 43 3	13 11
29	W	8 26 1	5 43 34	18 51	28 55 16	0 30	11 23	6✕ 1 32	9 26
30	Th	8 29 58	6 40 55	18 36	13✕ 1 30	0 S 47	7 24	19 54 56	5 17
31	F	8 33 55	7 38 17	18 22	26 41 46	1 59	3 8	3♈22 6	0 59

FIRST QUARTER—July 21, 5h. 12m. 33s. a.m.

Full Moon—July 27, 7h. 13m. 37s. p.m.

EPHEMERIS] **JULY, 1942.** 15

D M	Venus Lat. ° ′	Venus Declin. ° ′	Venus Declin. ° ′	Mercury Lat. ° ′	Mercury Declin. ° ′	Mercury Declin. ° ′	☽ Node. ° ′
1	1 S 46	19 N 15	19 N 30	3 S 51	19 N 8	19 N 20	7 ♍ 14
3	1 42	19 44	19 58	3 33	19 33	19. 46	7 8
5	1 38	20 11	20 23	3 11	20 0	20 15	7 1
7	1 33	20 36	20 47	2 48	20 30	20 45	6 55
9	1 29	20 58	21 9	2 23	21 0	21 14	6 49
11	1 24	21 19	21 28	1 57	21 29	21 43	6 42
13	1 19	21 37	21 46	1 30	21 56	22 8	6 36
15	1 14	21 53	22 0	1 4	22 20	22 29	6 30
17	1 9	22 7	22 13	0 38	22 38	22 44	6 23
19	1 4	22 19	22 23	0 12	22 49	22 52	6 17
21	0 58	22 27	22 31	0 N 12	22 52	22 50	6 10
23	0 53	22 34	22 36	0 34	22 45	22 38	6 4
25	0 47	22 38	22 39	0 53	22 28	22 16	5 58
27	0 42	22 39	22 39	1 10	22 1	21 43	5 51
29	0 36	22 38	22 37	1 24	21 23	21 0	5 45
31	0 30	22 34		1 34	20 34		5 39

Mutual Aspects.

1. ☉ ⊥ ♅. ♀ ✱ ♇. ♂ ⊥ ♃.
2. ☿ ∠ ♇. ♀ ⊻ ♃.
3. ♀ ☌ & P ♄. ♂ ∠ ♆. 4. ☿ P ♄
5. ☉ ⊥ ♄. 6. ☉ ⊻ ♂.
7. ☿ P ♅. ♀ P ♅.
8. ☉ Q ♆. ♂ Q ♅.
9. ☿ P ♀. 10. ☿ □ ♆.
11. ☉ ∠ ♅. 12. ☿ ⊥ ♇.
13. ☉ P ☿. ♀ ✱ ♂.
14. ☉ P ♀. ♀ ∠ ♇. 15. ☿ ⊻ ♅.
16. ☉ ∠ ♄. ☿ ∠ ♂, ⊻ ♇.
17. ♂ Q ♄.
18. ☿ ☌ ♃, ⊻ ♄, ⊥ ♅. ♂ ⊥ ♆.
20. ☉ P ♅, ✱ ♆. [♃ ⊻ ♄.
21. ☿ ⊥ ♄. ♀ □ ♆. [♃ ⊥ ♅.
22. ☉ ⊻ ♀. ☿ Q ♆. ♀ ⊥ ♇.
23. ☉ P ♄. ☿ ⊥ ♂, ∠ ♅.
24. ☿ P ♀: ♂ ∠ ♃.
26. ☿ ∠ ♄. ♀ ⊻ ♅.
27. ☉ ✱ ♅. ☿ ⊻ ♂. ♀ ⊻ ♇.
28. ☿ ✱ ♆. ♂ ⊻ ♆.
29. ☉ ☌ ♇. [⊥ ♅
31. ☿ ✱ & P ♅. ☿ ☌ ♇. ♀ ⊻ ♄,

	D M	♆ Long. ° ′	♅ Long. ° ′	♄ Long. ° ′	♃ Long. ° ′	♂ Long. ° ′	♀ Long. ° ′	☿ Long. ° ′	Lunar Aspects ☉	♇	♆	♅	♄	♃	♂	♀	☿
	1	27 ♍ 14	2 ♊ 39	6 ♊ 47	4 ♋ 48	10 ♌ 45	4 ♊ 12	18 ♊ 53	Q					Q			△
	2	27 15	2 42	6 54	5 2	11 22	5 23	19 28	△			□	□	△		□	
1942	3	27 16	2 45	7 1	5 16	11 59	6 33	20 8		Q							□
	4	27 17	2 48	7 8	5 29	12 36	7 44	20 53		△	☍	✱	✱	□	Q		
	S	27 18	2 51	7 14	5 43	13 14	8 55	21 42	□			∠			△	✱	
	6	27 18	2 54	7 21	5 57	13 51	10 6	22 36					∠			∠	✱
	7	27 19	2 57	7 28	6 10	14 28	11 16	23 34		□	Q	⊻	⊻	✱	□	⊻	∠
	8	27 20	2 59	7 35	6 24	15 6	12 27	24 37	✱					∠			⊻
	9	27 21	3 2	7 41	6 37	15 43	13 38	25 44	∠	✱	△	☌	☌	⊻			
	10	27 22	3 5	7 48	6 51	16 20	14 50	26 56	⊻	∠					✱	☌	
	11	27 23	3 7	7 54	7 4	16 58	16 1	28 11			□				∠		☌
	S	27 24	3 10	8 1	7 18	17 35	17 12	29 31		⊻		⊻	⊻	☌			
	13	27 25	3 13	8 7	7 32	18 12	18 23	0 ♋ 56	☌			∠	∠		⊻	⊻	
	14	27 27	3 15	8 14	7 45	18 50	19 34	2 24		☌	✱	✱	✱	⊻		∠	⊻
	15	27 28	3 18	8 20	7 58	19 27	20 46	3 56			∠				☌		∠
	16	27 29	3 21	8 26	8 12	20 5	21 57	5 32	⊻		⊻			∠		✱	
	17	27 30	3 23	8 33	8 25	20 42	23 8	7 12	∠	⊻		□	□	✱			✱
	18	27 31	3 25	8 39	8 39	21 20	24 20	8 55	✱	∠	☌				⊻	□	
	S	27 33	3 28	8 45	8 52	21 57	25 31	10 42		✱		△	△	□	∠		
	20	27 34	3 30	8 51	9 5	22 35	26 43	12 32				Q	Q		✱		□
	21	27 35	3 33	8 57	9 19	23 12	27 55	14 25	□	□	⊻					△	
	22	27 36	3 35	9 3	9 32	23 50	29 6	16 21			∠			△		Q	△
	23	27 38	3 37	9 9	9 45	24 27	0 ♋ 18	18 19	△	△	✱	☍		Q	□		Q
1963	24	27 39	3 39	9 15	9 58	25 5	1 30	20 19	Q	Q			☍				
64	25	27 41	3 42	9 20	10 11	25 43	2 42	22 21			□				△	☍	
65	S	27 42	3 44	9 26	10 25	26 20	3 54	24 24				Q		☍	Q		
	27	27 43	3 46	9 32	10 38	26 58	5 5	26 29	☍	☍	△	△	Q				☍
	28	27 45	3 48	9 37	10 51	27 35	6 17	28 35			Q		△				
	29	27 46	3 50	9 43	11 4	28 13	7 29	0 ♌ 41				□		Q	☍	Q	
	30	27 48	3 52	9 48	11 17	28 51	8 42	2 47					□	△		△	Q
	31	27 50	3 54	9 53	11 30	29 28	9 54	4 53	Q	Q	☍						

Last Quarter—July 5, 8h. 58m. 12s. a.m.

As the time given is Double Summer Time 2 hours must be *subtracted* to convert to G.M.T. Birth was 34 minutes after midnight on the morning of 4th July. Subtraction of 2 hours brings the time to 10.34 p.m. G.M.T., on the previous day, 3rd July. The new data we now have on which to base our calculations is:

> 10.34 p.m., G.M.T.
> 3rd July 1942
> Windsor (Lat. 51° 28'N; Long. 0° 36'W)

Let me just give an example of how we should go about converting to G.M.T. had this birth occurred at New York in the U.S.A. at 0.34 a.m. on the 4th July 1942. The longitude of New York is 74° west of Greenwich. Refer to the Standard Times in Appendix and we find New York State is 5 hours *slow* of G.M.T. Therefore we ADD 5 hours to the birth-time given = 0.34 a.m.+5 hours = 5.34 a.m. G.M.T.

Stage 2: finding the local sidereal time at birth

Why bother to find this? Because we want to know what are the Ascendant and M.C. of the chart, and to which houses the planets and signs will relate. Refer again to Chapter 6 for a definition of local sidereal time. The guiding link for us is given in the *Ephemeris* for the G.M.T. day of birth: local sidereal time for Greenwich at *noon* was 6h. 43m. 31s. on the 3rd July 1942. Refer to this month of the *Ephemeris* reproduced on pages 85–6. The first and second columns on the left show the 31 days of the month. The third column is headed *Sidereal Time*. Run your finger down to the 3rd day and you will read 6h. 43m. 31s. as the sidereal time at Greenwich for noon. We proceed as follows:

		H	M	S
Sidereal time noon G.M.T., 3rd July		= 6	43	31
Interval FROM noon to birth-time	(ADD)	= 10	34	00
Result		= 17	17	31
Acceleration on interval (10 secs of sidereal time for each hour of mean time)	(ADD)	=	1	44
Sidereal time at Greenwich at birth		= 17	19	15
Longitude Equivalent in Time	(SUBTRACT)	=	2	24
LOCAL SIDEREAL TIME AT BIRTH		= 17	16	51

Because birth was *p.m.* we ADD the interval from noon to birth (10 hours 34 minutes) to the sidereal time for noon G.M.T. which we took from the *Ephemeris* for the 3rd July. You are probably wondering what is the *acceleration on the interval*. This is an additional adjustment that has to be made because we are converting *mean time* into *sidereal time*. Remember what you read in Chapter 6 that the length of a sidereal day in *mean time* is 23h. 56m. 4s. approximately. For all practical purposes the difference is 4 minutes, or 240 seconds. If we divide 24 (hours) into 240 (seconds) the result is 10. Therefore, if birth G.M.T. is *p.m.*, for *every hour* of the interval from noon to birth-time we *add* 10 *seconds* of acceleration, and for *every 6 minutes* we *add 1 second*. If birth is *a.m.*, the interval is from the birth-time TO noon, and the acceleration on this interval is *subtracted*.

The *Longitude Equivalent in Time* refers to the difference in *time* between the place of birth and *Greenwich*, determined by their difference in longitude. The longitude of the birthplace is multiplied by 4 (because the Sun transits 1° of longitude in 4 minutes) and the answer is in minutes. If birthplace is *west* of Greenwich the Longitude Equivalent is *subtracted*, if *east* it is *added*.

The *local sidereal time* for our example birth we calculated as 17h. 16m. 51s. Our next step is to refer to a *Tables of Houses*. If you want to calculate other charts you will be buying a copy, so we will simply reproduce here a few lines taken from these Tables. We turn to the page for the *latitude* of birthplace. It is Windsor, latitude 51° 28′N. The nearest Tables are for 51° 32′N. (This is the latitude of London, and tables are actually given for London, Liverpool and New York in all *Raphael's Ephemerides*.) We find the sidereal time nearest to the local sidereal time of our chart.

	Sidereal Time	10 ♐	11 ♍	12 ♍	Ascen ♓		2 ♉	3 ♊
	H M S	°	°	°	°	′	°	°
Nearest earlier time:	17 16 29	20	8	29	4	40	2	0
Nearest later time:	17 20 49	21	9 ♒	0	7	2	3	1

If we do not want to be exact we use the degrees corresponding to the nearest sidereal time (17h. 16m. 29s.) to that of the local sidereal time at birth. The numbers at the top of each column are the numbers of the houses of the chart, 10th, 11th, 12th, Ascendant, 2nd, 3rd. The columns contain the signs and degrees on the cusps of these houses by the Placidean System. We are using Equal House, so we only want to know the sign and degree for the M.C. and Ascendant. In these Tables the 10 column is always the M.C. So from the above, corresponding approximately to our local sidereal time of 17h. 16m. 51s. we have an Ascendant of Pisces 4° 40', and a M.C. of Sagittarius 20°.

But perhaps we want to be more precise. We want to calculate the *exact* degrees and minutes corresponding to the local sidereal time. This is the formula:

Calculation of exact ascendant and M.C.[1]

	H M S		H M S
Nearest later time	= 17 20 49	Local sidereal time	= 17 16 51
Nearest earlier time	= 17 16 29	Nearest earlier time	= 17 16 29

$$\text{difference} = \quad 4\ 20 = A \qquad\qquad \text{difference} = \qquad 22 = B$$

A = 4m. 20s. or 260 seconds; B = 22 seconds.

| M.C. at later time | = ♐ 21° | Asc at later time | = ♓ 7° 2' |
| M.C. at earlier time | = ♐ 20° | Asc at earlier time | = ♓ 4° 40' |

$$\text{difference} = \quad 1° = C \qquad\qquad \text{difference} = \quad 2°\ 22' = D$$

C = 1° or 60 minutes; D = 2° 22' or 142 minutes.

Thus: $$\frac{B \times D}{A} = \frac{22 \times 142}{260} = 12 \text{ minutes.}$$

This answer of 12 minutes is added to the Ascendant corresponding to the nearest *earlier* sidereal time. Thus: Pisces 4° 40' + 12' = Ascendant Pisces 4° 52'. And for the M.C.:

$$\frac{B \times C}{A} = \frac{22 \times 60}{260} = 5 \text{ minutes.}$$

This answer of 5 minutes is added to the M.C. corresponding to the nearest *earlier* sidereal time. Thus: Sagittarius 20° + 5· = M.C. Sagittarius 20° 5'.

Beginners can ignore this exactness until later.

[1] With acknowledgments to Margaret Hone: *The Modern Textbook of Astrology.*

And so we have determined the two important angles of our example chart: Asc. ♓ 4° 52′; M.C. ♐ 20° 5′.

The next step is to insert these on our chart-form. Look at Figure 1. On the left hand side (eastern horizon) you will see the figures for our Ascendant. Near the top of the chart you will see an arrow indicating the M.C. Pisces 4° 52′ is the Ascendant or 1st house cusp, and this figure of 4° 52′ will be on *every* house cusp, only the sign changing each time. We always enter the sign and degree for the Ascendant first, and then insert the rest of the signs in their correct order *from* the Ascendant. Don't forget to mark in the dividing line between signs. Then enter the M.C. The basis for the chart is now fixed, ready for the planets to be entered.

Births in Southern Hemisphere. For births in the Southern Hemisphere there is a small additional calculation to determine the local sidereal time. Since any point in the Northern Hemisphere is separated from its opposite point in the Southern Hemisphere by 12 hours, we *add* 12 *hours* to what would for a birth in the Northern Hemisphere be its local sidereal time. As an example, let us use the figures for our example chart, assuming the latitude of Windsor to be 51° 28′ *South*.

		H	M	S
Local sidereal time at birth	=	17	16	51
ADD 12 hours	=	12		
		29	16	51
Subtract 24 hours	=	24		
		5	16	51

We subtract 24 hours whenever the 'hour' column exceeds 24, since sidereal time reaches 24 hours and then starts again from 0 hours. With these figures of 5h. 16m. 51s. we would turn to the latitude of 51° 32′ in the *Tables of Houses*, and when we have found the nearest sidereal time we *reverse* the corresponding *sign* of both Ascendant and M.C., but use the degrees and minutes as they are shown. For instance, our example chart has an Ascendant of Pisces 4° 52′. If this were for a Southern Hemisphere birth the Ascendant would be Virgo (opposite sign to Pisces) 4° 52′. Likewise the M.C., instead of being Sagittarius 20° 5′ would be Gemini 20° 5′.

It must be emphasised, however, that the signs in which the planets are placed are NOT reversed for Southern Hemisphere births. This is often a misunderstanding with beginners.

Stage 3: calculating the planets' positions

We will begin with the Sun, and calculate each planet's celestial longitude in turn. In each case you should refer to the July pages reproduced from the 1942 *Ephemeris*, from which the necessary figures will be taken, and to Appendix VI for the Logarithm Tables.

The first thing to consider is the birth-time. If it is *p.m.* we work forward FROM the noon of birthday. If *a.m.* we work forward from the noon of the *previous* day TO the noon of birthday. In the case of our example chart birth was 10.34 *p.m.*, so we work forward from noon of birthday.

In the 4th column for July 1942 you will see the heading, Long. Here are the longitudinal positions of the Sun for *noon* on each day of the month. We want to find out the distance in longitude (daily motion) travelled by the Sun in the 24 hours from noon on the 3rd July to noon on the 4th.

Sun's longitude noon 4th July = ♋ 11° 52′ (to nearest minute)
„   „   „ 3rd „   = ♋ 10° 55′ („   „   )
_____
Daily motion in 24 hours =   57′

Now we turn to Appendix VI, to the Proportional Logarithms. At the top, from 0 to 15 are degrees or hours. The first column, from top to bottom, indicates minutes of either mean time or celestial longitude, from 0 to 59.

First we find the Log. of the *interval*. You will remember this is 10 hours 34 minutes (from noon to birth-moment). Column '10' (top line) indicates 10 hours. Run your finger down this column until you come to the line corresponding to '34 minutes'. The Log. is ·3563. Now, in the same way, find the Log. for the Sun's motion (from noon 3rd to noon 4th) of 57′. Run your finger down column '0' until you come to line '57'. The Log. is 1·4025. We add these together:

Log. of interval   = ·3563
Log. of Sun's motion = 1·4025
_____
Addition of Logs.   = 1·7588

Looking at the Table of Logs. again we find the *nearest* figure to 1·7588. It is 1·7604, which corresponds to 0° 25′. This tells us that from noon on the 3rd July until the moment of birth at 10.34 p.m. the Sun travelled 25′ in celestial longitude. As birth is p.m. we ADD this 25′ to the noon position of the Sun given in the *Ephemeris* for the 3rd.

Sun's longitude noon 3rd July = ♋ 10° 55′
Sun's motion during interval   =   25′
────
Sun's longitude at birth   = ♋ 11° 20′

We calculate the Moon in the same way.

Moon's longitude noon 4th July = ♈   1° 32′ (to nearest minute)
„   „   „   3rd „   = ♓ 18° 22′ („   „   )
────
Moon's motion in 24 hours   =   13° 10′

Log. of interval   = ·3563
Log. of Moon's motion = ·2607
────
Addition of Logs.   = ·6170

Nearest figure in Tables of Logs. to ·6170 = ·6168 = 5° 48′

Moon's longitude noon 3rd July = ♓ 18° 22′
Moon's motion during interval   =   5° 48′
────
Moon's longitude at birth   = ♓ 24° 10′

Do you get the idea? Now for Mercury, Venus, Mars:

	☿	♀	♂
Noon position 4th July	= ♊ 20° 53′	♊ 7° 44′	♌ 12° 36′
„ „ 3rd „	= ♊ 20° 8′	♊ 6° 33′	♌ 11° 59′
Daily motion	= 45′	1° 11′	37
Log. of interval	= ·3563	·3563	·3563
Log. of motion	= 1·5051	1·3071	1·5902
Addition of Logs.	= 1·8614	1·6634	1·9465
Nearest figures in Tables	= 1·8573	1·6670	1·9542
Anti-log. of nearest figure	= 20′	31′	16′
ADD to noon position 3rd	= ♊ 20° 8′	♊ 6° 33′	♌ 11° 59
Longitude at birth	= ♊ 20° 28′	♊ 7° 4′	♌ 12° 15′

The remaining planets, Jupiter, Saturn, Uranus, Neptune and Pluto have a very small daily motion, so their motion during the interval can be easily worked out proportionately in one's head. The interval (10h. 34m.) is almost half of 24 hours.

Jupiter's motion 3rd–4th = 13′ and nearly half of this is 6′
Saturn's motion 3rd–4th = 7′ and nearly half of this is 3′
Uranus'   motion 3rd–4th = 3′ and nearly half of this is 1′
Neptune's motion 3rd–4th = 1′

	♃	♄	♅	♆
Noon position 3rd July	= ♋ 5° 16′	♊ 7° 1′	♊ 2° 45′	♏ 27° 16′
Motion during interval	=	6′	3′	1′	0′
Longitude at birth	= ♋ 5° 22′	♊ 7° 4′	♊ 2° 46′	♏ 27° 16′

Pluto's position at 10-day intervals throughout the year is given on page 39 of the 1942 *Ephemeris*. We assess its position for the 3rd July by proportion:

Pluto's longitude 10 July   = ♌ 4° 49′
   „   „   30th June = ♌ 4° 33′

Pluto's motion in 10 days   =   16′

By the 3rd July (⅓ of 10 days) Pluto had moved about 5′. Add this to Pluto's longitude on 30th June (♌ 4° 33′) and longitude for 3rd July becomes ♌ 4° 38′.

It so happens that at the time of the birth we are considering no planet was *retrograde*. Retrograde is when a planet, as seen from the Earth, appears to be moving *backwards* to its normal direct motion. This is not what is happening. It only *appears* so due to the angle of both the Earth and the planets in their orbits.[1] The following rules apply to the calculation of a *retrograde* planet's longitude:

(a) When birth is *a.m.* motion during interval is *added* to noon position;

(b) When birth is *p.m.* motion during interval is *subtracted* from noon position.

---

[1] Excellently illustrated in *The Astrologer's Astronomical Handbook*.

Moon's Nodes

         ☊ North Node   ☋ South Node

Just as the Sun's apparent path around the Earth intersects the equator at the equinoxes, so the Moon's apparent path around the Earth intersects the *ecliptic* at what are called the *nodes*. When the Moon crosses the ecliptic from south to north this is called the ascending or North Node; when it crosses from north to south this is called the descending or South Node. This *nodical revolution* of the Moon takes a little over 27 days. Each time it crosses the ecliptic at the same node this point has moved backwards along the ecliptic just a little, the complete cycle of 360° taking about 18 years 10 days.

This retrograde cycle of the Moon is similar in motion to the Precession of the Equinoxes, and the North Node may be likened to the First Point of Aries where the Sun crosses from south to north of the Earth's equator, and the South Node to the Libra equinox when the Sun descends from north to south. With this idea in mind astrologers have attempted to interpret these obviously important points in the Moon's cycle, in terms of human behaviour and activities. Although it is not yet evident that they are particularly vital factors in the chart the North Node, according to its placing by sign, house and aspects, seems to indicate a direction from which one might expect to receive benefits *through no conscious effort*; and the South Node, a direction from which life will *take away from one and demand effort and sacrifice without expected reward*. The South Node is often an indicator of ill-health, interpreted according to the part of the body associated with the sign involved.

If you refer to the July page of the 1942 *Ephemeris* near the right-hand corner (*Ephemeris* page 15) you will see a column headed '☽ Node'. This is the North Node. Its position changes only 3′ per day. At noon on the 3rd July it was in Virgo 7° 8′, so by 10.34 that day it would be about Virgo 7° 7′. The South Node always occupies exactly the opposite point in the ecliptic, in this case Pisces 7° 7′.

Inserting planets in chart. We can now list the planets and nodes by longitude ready to be written in the chart.

☉	Sun	♋	11° 20′
☽	Moon	♓	24° 10′
☿	Mercury	♊	20° 28′
♀	Venus	♊	7° 4′
♂	Mars	♌	12° 15′
♃	Jupiter	♋	5° 22′

♄	Saturn	♊	7° 4'
♅	Uranus	♊	2° 46'
♆	Neptune	♍	27° 16'
♇	Pluto	♌	4° 38'
☊	North Node	♍	7° 7'
☋	South Node	♓	7° 7'

Refer to Figure 1 and you will see how the planets and nodes should be placed against their respective signs of occupancy. Try to insert a planet near where its degree would be. For instance, Neptune is in 27° Virgo, 3° from the end of the sign – you would not therefore clumsily enter Neptune in the middle of the sign. One's prime aim must always be for accuracy and neatness, the chart attractive and easy to read. You should cover up Figure 1 and try setting up the example chart yourself.

Declinations of the Planets. The declination of a planet is its angular distance north or south of the equator, and is the second co-ordinate for determining a planet's position relative to the Earth. Turn again to the *Ephemeris* pages. You will see a column headed 'Dec.' for each planet. Only the Moon can move an appreciable distance in 24 hours, therefore needing to be calculated by Logs. You must be careful to note whether the Moon by declination is *decreasing* or *increasing*. When it is increasing it is moving *from* the equator towards maximum declination. When it is decreasing it is moving *towards* the equator from maximum declination. Our example chart birth occurred when the Moon was decreasing in declination, as you will note:

Moon's declination noon 3rd July   = 5° 38' S
,,   ,,   ,,   4th ,,   = 1° 26' S
_____
Moon's motion by declination   = 4° 12'
Log. of Moon's dec. motion (4° 12') = ·7570
Log. of interval   = ·3563
_____

Addition of Logs.   = 1·1133
Nearest figure to addition   = 1·1130 = 1° 51'
Moon's declination noon 3rd July = 5° 38' S
Moon's dec. motion during interval = 1° 51'   (subtract)
_____

Moon's declination at birth   = 3° 47' S

The rest of the planets' declinations can be calculated proportionately as we did with the longitudes of the slower-moving planets, and should be as follows:

☉	Sun	22° 58′ N		♄	Saturn	19° 46′ N
☿	Mercury	19° 39′ N		♅	Uranus	20° 33′ N
♀	Venus	19° 50′ N		♆	Neptune	2° 17′ N
♂	Mars	18° 19′ N		♇	Pluto	23° 39′ N
♃	Jupiter	23° 14′ N				
	and the Moon ☽		3° 47′ S			

Stage 4 in the calculation of the natal chart, the assessing of planetary aspects, will be dealt with in the next chapter.

Recommended further reading

This present book contains all that is necessary for you to learn how to calculate and erect a birth-chart. But for those readers who would wish to go further and to study in more detail, the following books by Jeff Mayo are highly recommended.

How to Read the Ephemeris.   Explains with the help of reproductions of eleven pages from *Raphael's Ephemeris* the various columns of data.

How to Cast a Natal Chart.   Written in great detail. Includes exercises at the end of most chapters; answers given.

The Astrologer's Astronomical Handbook.   See Appendix 1.

10

The aspects

An *aspect* is the angular distance measured along the ecliptic in degrees and minutes of celestial longitude between two points, as viewed from the Earth. In astrology, aspects are formed between any two planets, also between a planet and the Ascendant or M.C. Every planet in a chart is not in aspect with every other planet (I doubt whether this would ever occur). Only those planets separated by a certain measurement are considered as being in aspect.

The Aspects

Symbol	Exact Aspect	Name	Orb	Strength
☌	0°	conjunction	8°	powerful
∨	30°	semi-sextile	2°	slight
∟	45°	semi-square	2°	slight
✶	60°	sextile	6°	fairly strong
□	90°	square	8°	powerful
△	120°	trine	8°	powerful
⟗	135°	sesquiquadrate	2°	slight
⚻	150°	quincunx	2°	slight
☍	180°	opposition	8°	powerful
P	0°	parallel (of declination)	1½°	powerful

Why aspects? When two planets are separated by a certain number of degrees this combined angular relationship with the Earth is associated with significant effects upon life on Earth. This is very evident to anyone through the Moon's phases (conjunction, square, opposition, square) when the Sun-Moon angular relationship to the Earth has predictable tidal effects. An aspect between any two planets in an individual birth-chart corresponds with an *accentuation* of the characteristics associated with the principles of these planets, which can produce weak or strong psychological features.

Orbs. An *orb* is an allowance of so many degrees either side of an exact aspect. Two planets, therefore, can form an aspect even though their distance apart is not exactly that of the aspect angle, providing they are 'within orb'. E.g., Mars is in Aries 10°, Sun is in Leo 16°. They are 126° apart. If you refer to the list of aspects you will see that an *exact* trine aspect is 120° between two planets, but an orb of 8° is allowed. Sun-Mars are within 6° orb of exact trine aspect. To be within orb they could have been anywhere between 112°–128° apart. An astrologer does not write down the number of degrees separating two planets that are in aspect (e.g. 126°), but indicates the aspect by its symbol (in our example case △).

Conjunction (☌). A focal point, giving strong emphasis to the characteristics of the planets and signs involved. The principles of the planets will react to stimulus together, and on each other. E.g., ☿ ☌ ♀, mental reactions and feelings will function together.

Parallel (P). This is the only aspect not measured in celestial longitude. Two (or more) planets having the same angular distance *in declination*, measured in degrees and minutes, north or south from the celestial equator are parallel. Similar effects to the conjunction, if both planets same side of equator; as opposition if planets on opposite sides of equator.

Opposition (☍). Indicative of tension. In a positive way the planets and signs can be complementary, the characteristics of one supplementing those of the other. Stress will be evident if the characteristics of one are employed at the expense of the characteristics of the other. This aspect provides a key to the resolving of what could be an inner conflict of contrasting behaviour. It suggests the necessity for the *equal* development and exercise of complementary features in the make-up.

Trine (△). Indicative of inner harmony and ease of expression if the positive characteristics of *both* planets (and signs) are *equally* developed and exercised. Often indicative of a 'line of least resistance', especially with weak characters. A chart dominated by trines, perhaps forming one or more *Grand Trines* (Figure 9) can produce a person of weak character if success or material benefits come to them too easily and they make no personal effort to achieve an objective. A trine aspect to a planet that also receives a square from another planet, can point to ways of resolving the conditions aggravated by the square aspect.

Square (□). Indicative of frustration, disruption, inner conflict. But a source of energy and activation for someone determined to overcome misfortunes and personal weaknesses or inadequacies associated with this factor. Frequently one comes upon the chart of a successful and powerful character that is dominated by square aspects. Again it must be stressed that the positive characteristics of *both* planets (and signs) must be *equally* developed and exercised for this to be a source of constructive power. Weak characters can be easily wrecked and their attitude to life unbalanced by powerful squares.

Sextile (✶). Similar to the trine but of less significance.

Semi-sextile, Semi-square, Sesquiquadrate, Quincunx (⊻ ⌐ ⌑ ⊼). Of minor importance, suggestive of features in the chart productive of slight strain, and where a conscious positive attitude will be required (i.e., in development of the characteristics of the planets and signs involved, and affairs of the houses emphasised).

Grand Trine. A pattern formed by three trine aspects involving three or more planets (Figure 9). If positively responded to, productive of a person at ease within himself. See also under *trine*.

Grand Cross. A pattern formed by two pairs of opposing planets involving four squares (Figure 9). An intensification of the definition for a single square aspect. Often proves to be a 'make or break' pattern: either the person develops unusual ability or strength of character, or he feels crushed and that fate has given him more than his fair share of hardship and frustration. Possibly it is found mostly in charts of those of us who fall in between the two extremes, who never achieve anything in life without that or something else ultimately being taken from us. If this pattern falls across *Fixed* signs it usually denotes one who accepts and makes the best of misfortune, though it can produce chronic health conditions. If across *Cardinal* signs the person is most likely to endeavour to overcome afflictions. If across *Mutable* signs, though the person may try to by-pass difficulties, this can lead to greater confusion, frustration and nervous reaction because the conditions have not been superseded by strength of character in overcoming them.

T-Square. A pattern formed by two planets in opposition, each square to a third planet. The tension typical of the opposition is aggravated by the additional problems introduced by the third afflicting planet. A combination of both aspects.

Unaspected planet. This does not mean the planet is a weak factor

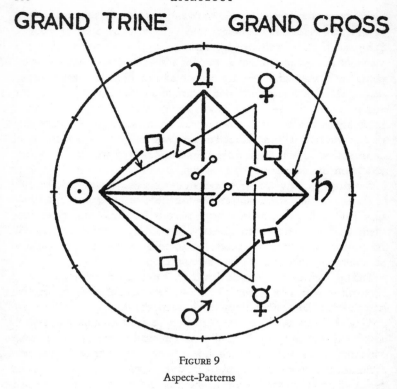

FIGURE 9
Aspect-Patterns

in the chart. Usually it is indicative, according to the planet, sign and house involved, of characteristics or a feature in the life of the person which it is difficult, or perhaps not attempted, to integrate with the rest of the nature or life-pattern.

A guide to interpretation of aspects. Astrologers sometimes wonder why aspects often produce different effects to those they expected. This could show lack of understanding of the basic function of aspects.

An aspect brings the principles of two planets together. The characteristics associated with both planets (and signs involved) must be *equally* developed, and employed *together*, if the function symbolised by the aspect is to be a powerful, constructive and healthy feature. Whatever the aspect it can prove either a beneficial or inharmonious factor, dependent upon the positive or negative reaction of the person concerned.

The presence in the chart of a square or opposition aspect indicates a possible 'weak link' in the nature or life-pattern, and it will *always* require much effort and perseverance to develop this feature into a source of energy and strength. Yet ultimately, a square positively used can prove that it has helped to 'make a man of character and achievement', whilst a trine aspect can easily 'make a man a lazy and parasitical flop'.

No aspect can be accurately assessed on its own, but must be considered with the pattern of the chart as a whole.

An absence of an aspect between two planets is often an important indication of character, if one remembers that planets represent vital life-principles, and that *wholeness of being* is achieved by the integration of each principle. The fact that a person always falls short of achieving an objective may be that two strong planets in his chart are unaspected together, lack necessary cohesion – e.g., the enterprise of Mars as Ascendant-Ruler, lacks the control and perseverance of Saturn, because the two are unaspected together in a chart.

The more *exact* an aspect, the stronger will be its effect.

An aspect will be stronger when the faster-moving planet of the pair is *applying* to the slower-moving planet (i.e., coming closer to the exact aspect), than when it is *separating* (the moment of exactness is passed). A planet will be faster-moving than another planet when its daily motion is greater, as can easily be seen from the *Ephemeris*.

Finding the aspects. There are various ways of finding the aspects, and any method is good if it is straightforward and is foolproof against overlooking an aspect. Refer to the example chart (Figure 1) and the classification of its aspects in Figure 10 and see if you can follow exactly how these aspects were assessed. Draw a 'box' similar to that in Figure 10, but without the aspects shown. See if *you* can find every aspect. Start with the Sun, seeing first if there are any planets *in orb* of conjunction, then count forward the exact number of degrees of each aspect (in the order shown in the list of aspects). When you have gone forward 180°, covering one half of the chart, proceed in the same way *backwards* from the Sun. When you find two planets do *not* form an aspect, place a small dot in their respective 'square', as indicated in Figure 10, in every case where there is no aspect. After completing your assessment of the Sun, do the Moon, then Mercury, and so on. Enter the aspects by celestial longitude in one half of the 'box'; in the other half enter any *parallel* aspects, allowing only an orb of 1½° in declination.

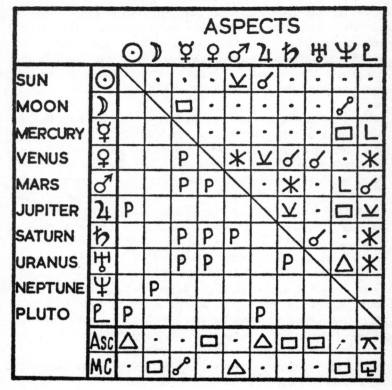

FIGURE 10
Aspects classified for Linda's birth-chart

Aspect-Lines. You will notice in the example chart (Figure 1) a pattern of lines drawn between the planets. The *thick* lines join planets that are in square or opposition aspect together; the *thin* lines join planets that are in sextile or trine aspect; *broken* lines join planets in minor aspect. It is a good idea to use different colours. I use an old pair of compasses (with a pencil in one end): stick the point in the centre of the wheel and mark a tiny pencil dot against each planet. When two planets are in aspect together it is then a neat and simple job to run a line between their respective 'dots'.

Once you are able to set up a chart quickly, you will find that you don't need to write down the planet's aspects – this aspect-pattern shows you immediately what are the aspects in the chart. You will learn to recognise certain patterns as a general indication of the direction of strain, ease, or unbalance, in the psychological sense.

Enter aspect-lines on the chart at the same time that you write the symbol in the 'aspect-box'. You can if you wish enter aspect-lines to Ascendant and M.C., though it is not normally done.

In the following definition of aspects it is important to remember that the basic impulse (reaction between the two aspected planets) *given for the conjunction* applies to the other aspects, but with less *concentrative* effect, and with probable *ease* of expression (easy aspects), and probable *difficulty* of expression (difficult aspects).

Easy aspects refer to the trine and sextile; *difficult*, to the square and opposition in particular, and to a much less extent the minor aspects (⊻ ∟ ⊡ ⊼).

Aspects of the Sun

The principle of a planet aspected by the Sun will *always* be emphasised as an important feature to be employed in the constructive and purposeful *integration* of the whole life and character.

Sun-Ascendant. *Conjunction:* develops a powerful personality-attitude, accentuating the Ascendant characteristics. *Easy:* Ascendant characteristics less dominant as for conjunction, but produce strong sense of inner harmony and self-confidence. *Difficult:* tendency to personality clash with other people.

Sun-M.C. *Conjunction:* develops a powerful Ego-complex, and urge to establish one's identity. *Easy:* less powerful Ego; with better success. *Difficult:* with resultant conflict of Ego with others and with one's whole nature.

Sun-Moon (☉-☽). *Conjunction:* develops powerful instinctive and emotional reactions; tendency to formation of deep-rooted habits; intense activity of energy can produce chronic disorders if suppressed, lowering resistance to impact of exterior life and to development of self-centred complexes; creativeness. *Easy:* with better prospects of instinctive harmony in emotional response and adjustment; success factor in development of private and business activities. *Difficult:* with probable inner conflict through uncertainty, restlessness, frustration; emotional disharmony and sensitivity.

Sun-Mercury (☉-☿). *Conjunction only:* develops powerful mental and nervous activity; good self-expression and mental ability if supported by other factors, otherwise possible lack of co-ordination of faculties, and nervous upsets; often unsettled, desirous of change.

Sun-Venus (☉-♀). *Conjunction:* develops powerful feelings, need to form sympathetic relationships; artistic and creative interest; strong sense of values; love of pleasure, human intimacy; needs affection. *Semi-sextile, semi-square:* much less evident, and feelings could be mis-applied or bring disappointments.

Sun-Mars (☉-♂). *Conjunction:* develops powerful self-expression, assertiveness, sexual and passionate urges; energetic and active, ad-venturous, enterprising; much courage, initiative, combativeness; accident-prone. *Easy:* with better prospects of controlled expression. *Difficult:* lacking control of energy; tendency to be reckless, over-impulsive, impatient, aggressive, forceful, over-sexed, of extremist attitude.

Sun-Jupiter (☉-♃). *Conjunction:* develops powerful self-expansive impulses; optimistic, good-humoured, generous, just and harmonious patterns of behaviour; conscientious, opportunist. *Easy:* with greater opportunity for successful self-expression. *Difficult:* with greater strug-gle to achieve desired expression and results; test of conscience; tend-ency to extravagance, exaggeration, conceit, serious misjudgments, false sense of superiority.

Sun-Saturn (☉-♄). *Conjunction:* develops powerful self-disciplinary patterns of behaviour and self-consciousness; cool and calculating, re-sponsible, practical, realist, resourceful; concentration and persistence of effort; sense of personal inadequacy and limitation; much patience, caution, reserve; depressive and worrying moods; introspective. *Easy:* with wiser acceptance and utilisation of limitations. *Difficult:* with greater struggle to overcome limitations; tendency to deep-rooted inhi-bitions, pessimism, self-pity, needless worrying, selfishness, fears and phobias, chronic ill-health.

Sun-Uranus (☉-♅). *Conjunction:* develops powerful deviations from the normal in self-expression; original, independent, disruptive, rebellious behavioural-patterns; usually an eventful life with dramatic changes, unsettlement; unorthodox, reformative tendencies. *Easy:* better prospects of developing unusual qualities as genius. *Difficult:* with emphasis on the drastic, dramatic, rebellious, self-willed be-havioural-patterns, tending to perversity, eccentricity, hysteria and 'misdirected genius'.

Sun-Neptune (☉-♆). *Conjunction:* develops powerful self-refining impulses and subtlety of expression; idealistic, impressionable, sensitive, impractical; attracted to creative and artistic pursuits, mysticism, emotional and sensual experience; escapist tendencies; should avoid drug and alcohol habits. *Easy:* with better prospects of directing gifts into constructive channels. *Difficult:* with tendency to self-deception, confusion, deceitfulness, scheming, neurotic reactions or forms of escape from fears and realities of life.

Sun-Pluto (☉-♇). *Conjunction:* develops powerful transforming or regenerative impulses; deep-rooted unconscious psychological features at critical stages in the life, producing an obsessional neurosis if resisted. *Easy:* with easier acceptance of the required transformation. *Difficult:* with greater difficulty of elimination, and in extreme cases, violent re-action.

Aspects of the Moon

A person's *instinctive and emotional response*, and the urge towards *formation of habits*, will be affected by the principle of a planet aspected by the Moon.

Moon-Ascendant. *Conjunction:* develops a responsive, emotional, habit-forming, yet restless side to the personality-attitude. *Easy:* blends the response characteristic of the sign Moon is in. *Difficult:* with an underlying emotional discord.

Moon-M.C. *Conjunction:* develops a responsive Ego-complex, increasing the sensitivity and emotional content. *Easy:* blends the characteristic response of the sign Moon is in. *Difficult:* with an underlying emotional discord.

Moon-Mercury (☽-☿). *Conjunction:* develops responsive mental and nervous activity; assimilative, good memory, sensitive, alert; need variety and change. *Easy:* with prospect of greater harmony of mental, emotional, nervous expression. *Difficult:* quick response, but indecisive, worrying, nervously restless, poor memory.

Moon-Venus (☽-♀). *Conjunction:* develops responsive feelings; friendly, popular, very affectionate; good sense of rhythm and balance; creative, artistic interest. *Easy:* less changeableness in feelings. *Difficult:* with possibility of unhappiness through affairs of the heart; awkwardness in expressing feelings; possible slovenly and immoral habits.

Moon-Mars (☽-♂). *Conjunction:* develops energetic and swift response; emotions and passions quickly roused; keen likes and dislikes; robust, restless, impatient. *Easy:* with less impatience, better self-control. *Difficult:* very indiscreet, intolerant, impulsive, forceful, passionate.

Moon-Jupiter (☽-♃). *Conjunction:* develops a responsive, self-expansive disposition; generous, sympathetic, protective, sociable. *Easy:* with increased geniality and instinctive judgment. *Difficult:* very responsive, self-expansive, but exaggerated behaviour; extravagant, careless, unstable emotions.

Moon-Saturn (☽-♄). *Conjunction:* develops self-disciplined, cool, and reserved response; shy, emotionally inhibited, depressive moods; rigid, deep-rooted habits through self-denial or fear of exposing personal limitations; underlying lack of confidence. *Easy:* better prospect of sensibly regulated habits. *Difficult:* with greater sensitivity, limited response; emotional disappointments and misunderstandings; very self-conscious; deep depressive moods.

Moon-Uranus (☽-♅). *Conjunction:* develops unusual, original forms of response; very changeable, restless, highly-strung, galvanic, emotionally-charged. *Easy:* with purposeful, progressive changes. *Difficult:* possibly perverse, over-excitable, eccentric, drastic, with many upheavals especially in family life.

Moon-Neptune (☽-♆). *Conjunction:* develops refined, subtle response and extreme emotional sensitivity; psychic, imaginative, artistic. *Easy:* with greater creative potential. *Difficult:* with probable confused, chaotic results, unstable emotions, deceitful, often neurotic and escapist tendencies.

Moon-Pluto (☽-♇). *Conjunction:* not a factor of consciousness; indicates probability of instinctive response to developments that will bring about ultimate changes of necessity, especially involving home or family. *Easy:* such changes achieved without much difficulty. *Difficult:* much upheaval through such changes.

Aspects of Mercury

A person's *communicative ability*, and the quality of *mental and nervous co-ordination* of the body and mind, will be affected by the principle of a planet aspected by Mercury.

Mercury-Ascendant. *Conjunction:* develops a mentally and nervously-active personality-attitude; restlessness. *Easy:* blends the characteristic mental and nervous attitude of sign Mercury is in. *Difficult:* with underlying mental and nervous disharmony and excitability.

Mercury-M.C. *Conjunction:* develops a mentally and nervously-active Ego-complex. *Easy:* blends the characteristic mental and nervous attitude of sign Mercury is in. *Difficult:* with underlying mental and nervous disharmony and excitability.

Mercury-Venus (☿-♀). *Conjunction:* mental and nervous activity stimulated by the feelings; charm, gentleness, agreeable and harmonious disposition. *Sextile:* with better prospect of harmony of expression. *Semi-sextile, semi-square:* probable slight changeableness and indiscretion through the affections.

Mercury-Mars (☿-♂). *Conjunction:* quick, assertive mental and nervous expression and reactions, stimulated by emotion and passion; forthright, enterprising, incisive. *Easy:* with more constructive thinking, stronger nervous system. *Difficult:* with tendency to overstrain, irritability, argumentativeness, sarcasm, recklessness.

Mercury-Jupiter (☿-♃). *Conjunction:* optimistic, expansive mental expression, strong nervous system; good judgment, thoughtful, philosophical. *Easy:* with good humour, wider opportunity for success in mental pursuits. *Difficult:* with careless judgment, exaggeration.

Mercury-Saturn (☽-♄). *Conjunction:* limited, disciplined mental expression, coolly regulated nervous reactions; profound, logical, calculated, depressive thinking. *Easy:* with better prospect of 'calculated' success. *Difficult:* with extreme lack of confidence, apprehension, prejudice, procrastination, severe depression and melancholia.

Mercury-Uranus (☿-♅). *Conjunction:* original and disruptive mental expression, high-strung nervous system; inventive, perceptive, scientifically-inclined, dramatic. *Easy:* with less nervous tension. *Difficult:* with tendency to eccentricity, extremist ideas, perversity, nervous 'spasms'.

Mercury-Neptune (☿-♆). *Conjunction:* subtlety, sensitivity of mental expression, easily disturbed nervous system; intuitive, idealistic, imaginative, refined, impressionable, vague. *Easy:* with better prospect of harmony of expression. *Difficult:* with tendency to confused thinking, absent-mindedness, dishonesty, vague fears and imaginings.

Mercury-Pluto (☿-♇). *Conjunction:* a need to consciously throw off worries and fears, eliminate disturbing thoughts, lest these become obsessions, deep-rooted neuroses, acute nervous tension. *Easy:* with better results, normal release of nervous tension. *Difficult:* tendency to explosive moods.

Aspects of Venus

A person's *feelings and affections, sense of personal values, and ability to form intimate relationships*, will be affected by the principle of a planet aspected by Venus.

Venus-Ascendant. *Conjunction:* develops an affectionate, friendly, artistic personality-attitude, with strong feelings. *Easy:* blends the characteristic sympathies and feeling attitude of the sign Venus is in. *Difficult:* with underlying disharmony and disappointments through the feelings and personal relations.

Venus-M.C. *Conjunction:* develops an affectionate, friendly, artistically-inclined Ego-complex. *Easy:* blends the characteristic sympathies and feeling attitude of sign Venus is in. *Difficult:* with underlying disharmony and disappointments through the feelings and personal relations.

Venus-Mars (♀-♂). *Conjunction:* active, impulsive, passionate feelings and sensual nature; quickly forms ties of affection; demonstrative; strong sex nature. *Easy:* with better prospect of co-operation with others. *Difficult:* with discontent, very erotic impulses, excessive passion, unhappy emotional relationships.

Venus-Jupiter (♀-♃). *Conjunction:* generous, expansive feeling nature, ardent affections; charm, popularity; good understanding of values, beauty, harmony. *Easy:* with better prospects of successful expression. *Difficult:* with extravagant or vulgar tastes, exaggerated feelings, vanity.

Venus-Saturn (♀-♄). *Conjunction:* limited or disciplined feelings, coolly affectionate; disappointments in love, delayed marriage; strict values; faithful. *Easy:* better control, rather than inadequacy, of feelings. *Difficult:* with selfish and exacting feelings; loneliness.

Venus-Uranus (♀-♅). *Conjunction:* abnormal or very excitable feelings, unusual tastes, unconventional values; artistic talent; magnetic charm, independent, romantic; tendency to illicit or broken love affairs, separations. *Easy:* with better prospect of successful expression. *Difficult:* with perverse feelings, very loose morals.

Venus-Neptune (♀-♆). *Conjunction:* refined, delicate feelings; self-deception, confusion, disillusionment through affections; idealistic, sentimental; great sense of harmony, rhythm, beauty, especially through music, poetry. *Easy:* with better prospect of successful expression. *Difficult:* greater risk of scandal, deception, through unreliable associates.

Venus-Pluto (♀-♇). *Conjunction:* a need to eliminate disturbing feelings, lest these become obsessional and neurotic tendencies. *Easy:* with better results, normal release of undesired feelings. *Difficult:* tendency to explosive feelings.

Aspect of Mars

A person's urge for *energetic, passionate or emotional expression* will be affected by the principle of a planet aspected by Mars.

Mars-Ascendant. *Conjunction:* develops an assertive, energetic personality-attitude, with strong passions and emotions. *Easy:* blends the characteristic energetic and emotional attitude of sign Mars is in. *Difficult:* with underlying emotional disharmony, fiery temper, forcefulness.

Mars-M.C. *Conjunction:* develops an assertive, energetic, emotionally-inclined Ego-complex. *Easy:* blends the characteristic energetic and emotional attitude of sign Mars is in. *Difficult:* with underlying emotional disharmony, fiery temper, forcefulness.

Mars-Jupiter (♂-♃). *Conjunction:* assertive, self-expansive impulses and activity; great enthusiasm, sportive, adventurous, generous, frank; ability to actively enjoy life. *Easy:* with better prospect of successful expression; often superiority complex, religious ideals. *Difficult:* with extremist tendencies, restless emotionalism, discontentment, wastefulness, boastfulness, bullying, gambling.

Mars-Saturn (♂-♄). *Conjunction:* self-assertive, disciplined, formative impulses, with limited or controlled emotion; constructive or destructive energy; self-reliant, practical, materialistic, hard, severe, ambitious. *Easy:* with better prospect of successful expression, executive ability. *Difficult:* with violent, cruel, unscrupulous behavioural-patterns, brute force, selfishness.

Mars-Uranus (♂-♅). *Conjunction:* energetic, enterprising impulses deviating from the normal; rebellious passions, excitable emotions; erratic self-will, restless, impatient, impulsive, fanatical courage; high nervous tension; tendency to sexual abnormalities. *Easy:* with better prospect of successful expression. *Difficult:* with tendency to eccentricity, irritability, extreme self-will.

Mars-Neptune (♂-♆). *Conjunction:* energetic, sensitive self-refining impulses; emotionally-coloured imagination; irrational fears; tendency to sexual, sensation-seeking, or religiose emotional patterns. *Easy:* enthusiasms successfully directed; creative inspirations. *Difficult:* with increased mental-emotional confusion, self-deception.

Mars-Pluto (♂-♇). *Conjunction:* a need to transform excess emotional and passional energies into constructive expression, unless these become eliminative processes of explosive temper or violence. *Easy:*

with better controlled release of excess energies. *Difficult:* greater difficulty in controlling these energies.

Aspects between Jupiter, Saturn, Uranus, Neptune and Pluto

Important Note. Aspects between these planets are within orb for
such long periods that unless either planet concerned is of a particularly personal significance in the chart, i.e., is on an angle, in close major
aspect with Sun, Moon or Mercury, or rules the sign in which is placed
either the Ascendant, Sun or Moon, these aspects can only be considered as indicating a *collective unconscious attitude* typical of everyone
born within a certain period.

Aspects of Jupiter

A person's urge for *expansion through growth, materially and by understanding*, will be affected by the principle of a planet aspected by
Jupiter.

Jupiter-Ascendant. *Conjunction:* develops a self-expansive, generous personality-attitude. *Easy:* blends the characteristic mode of self-
expansion of sign Jupiter is in. *Difficult:* with underlying exaggerative,
extravagant behaviour.

Jupiter-M.C. *Conjunction:* develops a self-expansive, generous,
understanding Ego-complex. *Easy:* blends the characteristic mode of
self-expansion of sign Jupiter is in. *Difficult:* with underlying, exaggerative, extravagant, self-opinionated attitude.

Jupiter-Saturn (♃-♄). The conjunction recurs about every 21
years. *Conjunction:* self-expansion through restricted, conformative
patterns of disciplined behaviour; growth of consciousness through response to religious, ˙materialistic, scientific, philosophical impulses.
Easy: with better prospect of successful expression, and understanding
of own limitations and compensating qualities. *Difficult:* losses, frustration, through inability to accept own limitations, or to make opportune use of compensating qualities.

Jupiter-Uranus (♃-♅). The conjunction recurs about every 14
years. *Conjunction:* self-expansion through deviations from the normal
in thought and ideas; growth of consciousness through response to
progressive, modernising, humanitarian, scientific impulses. *Easy:* with
better prospect of successful expression. *Difficult:* with tendency to in-
judicious, drastic anti-social compensations for personal inadequacies.

Jupiter-Neptune (♃-Ψ). The conjunction recurs about every 13 years. *Conjunction:* self-expansion through refined, creative, intuitive perceptiveness; growth of consciousness through response to devotional, mystical, artistic, philosophical impulses. *Easy:* with better prospect of successful expression. *Difficult:* with tendency to scatter-brained, escapist, emotionally-charged, sensation-seeking compensations for personal inadequacies.

Jupiter-Pluto (♃-♇). The conjunction recurs about every 13 years. *Conjunction:* self-expansion through the ability to make new beginnings from existing 'worn out' conditions. *Easy:* with better prospect of successful expression. *Difficult:* with tendency to destructive, drastic, obsessional forms of compensation for personal inadequacies.

Aspects of Saturn

A person's urge for *self-disciplined, self-conscious, regulated behaviour, and sense cf personal inadequacy*, will be affected by the principle of a planet aspected by Saturn.

Saturn-Ascendant. *Conjunction:* develops a limited, cautious, practical personality-attitude, impassive and reserved. *Easy:* blends the characteristic mode of self-control of sign Saturn is in. *Difficult:* with underlying lack of self-confidence, hardness, negativity.

Saturn-M.C. *Conjunction:* develops a limited, disciplined, matter-of-fact, ambitious Ego-complex. *Easy:* blends the characteristic mode of self-control of sign Saturn is in. *Difficult:* with underlying lack of self-confidence, hardness, negativity.

Saturn-Uranus (♄-♅). The conjunction recurs about every 46 years. *Conjunction:* ambitious, determined self-will, practical, mechanical-minded; alternating depressive and nervously-tensed moods. *Easy:* with better prospects of successful expression. *Difficult:* with tendency to egotism, cruelty.

Saturn-Neptune (♄-Ψ). The conjunction recurs about every 36 years. *Conjunction:* idealistic, creative impulses given form and practical purpose; or confused, impractical-thinking brings losses, inhibition of creative potential. *Easy:* with better prospect of successful expression. *Difficult:* with tendency to acute emotional frustration, deep neuroses.

Saturn-Pluto (♄-♇). The conjunction recurs about every 32 years. *Conjunction:* frustration could produce deep-rooted obsessional tendencies, with resultant eruptive or violent behaviour (due to conflicting factors: Saturn's restrictiveness, Pluto's getting-rid-of-ness). *Easy:*

better prospects for controlled and sensible rejection of conflicting factors. *Difficult:* with greater difficulty of control.

Aspects of Uranus

A person's urge to *deviate from the normal* through *originality, independence and inventiveness* will be affected by the principle of a planet aspected by Uranus.

Uranus-Ascendant. *Conjunction:* develops a magnetic, original, unusual, independent personality-attitude, with much nervous tension. *Easy:* blends the characteristic mode of originality of sign Uranus is in. *Difficult:* with underlying eccentric, rebelliously unconventional and erratic traits.

Uranus-M.C. *Conjunction:* develops an original, unusual, independent Ego-complex. *Easy:* blends the characteristic mode of originality of sign Uranus is in. *Difficult:* with underlying eccentric, rebelliously unconventional and erratic traits.

Uranus-Neptune (♅-♆). The conjunction recurs about every 171 years. *Conjunction:* the imaginative, inventive, scientifically-inclined mental faculties, combine with the subtle, intuitive, spiritually-inspired impressions and creativity; much emotional and mental sensitivity and nervous tension. *Easy:* with better prospects of successful expression. *Difficult:* tendency to self-deception, neurotic conditions.

Uranus-Pluto (♅-♇). The conjunction recurs about every 115 years. Develops characteristics of potentially dynamic creativeness or violent destructiveness, deep-rooted in all born in the period of about 10 years during which the aspect would be in orb. The *easy* aspects would tend to direct these energies into constructive channels with less inner tension and conflict than through the *difficult* or *conjunction* aspects.

Aspects of Neptune

A person's urge for *self-refinement*, and *creative and spiritual experience*, will be affected by the principle of a planet aspected by Neptune.

Neptune-Ascendant. *Conjunction:* develops a sensitive, artistic, out of the ordinary personality-attitude, with much nervous-emotional tension. *Easy:* blends the characteristic mode of impressionability of sign Neptune is in. *Difficult:* with underlying confusion, self-deception and neurotic tendencies.

Neptune-M.C. *Conjunction:* develops a sensitive, artistic, out of the ordinary Ego-complex, with much nervous-emotional tension. *Easy:*

blends the characteristic mode of impressionability of sign Neptune is in. *Difficult:* with underlying confused, self-deceptive and neurotic tendencies.

Neptune-Pluto (Ψ-Ε). Develops characteristics of a very subtle and deep-rooted type. The aspects are in orb over so very many years that they have the most generalised or 'collective' effects among the planetary aspects. It may be that essential new forms of 'spiritual awareness' in man are brought slowly yet inevitably 'to the surface' of his conscious mind during the long and critical periods marked by these aspects. The Neptune-Pluto process would undoubtedly produce much confusion, chaos and disintegration of accepted patterns of behaviour before establishing the required new feature of evolutionary growth in man.

Aspects of Pluto

A person's urge for *transforming* that which is not wanted into a new form of experience, will be affected by the principle of a planet aspected by Pluto.

Pluto-Ascendant. *Conjunction:* indicates the possibility of critical periods of upheaval during the life, when new beginnings, totally new experiences, have to be reshaped out of the destruction of the existing life-pattern; the *easy* aspects suggests likelihood of these transformations occurring without too much upset; the *difficult* aspects suggest inevitable strain upon the individual.

Pluto-M.C. The same indications apply here, though it is more likely the new beginnings will involve the individual's business or career interests than his more personal life, as would be the case with Pluto-Ascendant.

11

Planets in signs and houses

Interpretation of a chart can be confusing for a beginner because of the many factors to be considered and blended together, and there is no real short-cut to learning how to do this. First you must take the trouble to learn the keywords associated with planets, signs and houses, which will help you to expand in your own way the essential meaning or principle suggested by these keywords.

You will never be able to interpret the *unique features* symbolised in a chart if you always have to refer to a book for what the various factors indicate. Until you *understand* each factor, without having to refer to a textbook, you will not be in a position to judge astrology's essential value or to achieve the fullest benefit from its indications.

In this chapter you will be given a guide to the way you must *think* of a planet when it is placed in each sign and house. Space does not permit a fuller interpretation, yet even with these brief definitions you should be able to compile a remarkable caricature likeness to any person, known or unknown to you, based on their birth-data.

Keyword examples are given of each planet in a sign and house. Although these may read rather stilted it is an excellent method that simplifies interpretation. If you refer to each chapter dealing with the particular planet, sign or house, and carefully expand upon these keywords, you will quickly find you can compile your own interpretation of any permutated factors in a chart. What is more, you will realise these interpretations *do* apply to the person concerned!

The alternative definition given for a planet in a sign is the suggested *negative* reaction, often more apparent when the planet is *afflicted by aspect*.

THE SUN

Principle: self-integration.

By Sign: shows the characteristic way in which one can best integrate the contrasting, weak and strong, features in one's overall make-up, and aim to resolve major problems.

By House: emphasises the sphere of experience through which one can best learn self-integration, whether one desires these experiences or not.

Keywords Example: Sun in Gemini in 2nd house.

The principle of *self-integration* will function *adaptively*, *variably*, focusing on *possessions and personal security*.

Suggested Interpretation: An adaptive, restless and versatile nature that will instinctively seek in a variety of ways to satisfy the need for completeness of being or self-integration. This will focus a particular interest on the accumulation of possessions, and the contriving of ingenious methods for achieving personal security and monetary gain.

Sun in:

Aries (☉ ♈): assertive, enterprising, bold, singleness of purpose; or, combative, brusque, forceful, selfish.

Taurus (☉ ♉): practical, resourceful, conservative, productive; or, possessive, stubborn, self-indulgent.

Gemini (☉ ♊): adaptable, communicative, versatile, inquisitive; or, diffuse, restlessly excitable, inconstant, superficial.

Cancer (☉ ♋): shrewd, resourceful, sensitive, protective; or, touchy, self-pitying, retiring, over-emotional.

Leo (☉ ♌): powerful, impressive, dignified, loves to lead; or, bombastic, boastful, snobbish.

Virgo (☉ ♍): discriminating, practical, critical, efficient; or, fussy, worrisome, interfering.

Libra (☉ ♎): easy-going, peace-loving, friendly, artistic; or, lacking confidence, indecisive, delicate, lazy.

Scorpio (☉ ♏): intense, passionate, secretive, endurance; or, brooding, vindictive, obstinate.

Sagittarius (☉ ♐): free-ranging, optimistic, enthusiastic, idealistic; or, extravagant, exaggerating, restless, inconsiderate.

Capricorn (☉ ♑): practical, calculating, reserved, responsible; or, inhibited, slow, selfish, worrisome.

Aquarius (☉ ♒): detached, independent, reformative, idealistic; or, unconventional, erratic, rebellious.

Pisces (☉ ♓): sympathetic, impressionable, artistic, emotional, or, impractical, secretive, deceitful, timid.

THE MOON

Principle: rhythms.

By Sign: shows the mode of instinctive response to life and people on the nervous-emotional level: type of habits formed.

By House: emphasises the sphere of experience in which one will have a special interest, and which will influence *changes* of habit or residence.

Keywords Example: Moon in Taurus in 3rd house.

The principle of *rhythms* through instinctive response, assimilation, reflection will function *productively, enduringly*, focusing on *relationship of self to environment.*

Suggested Interpretation: A person whose manner of response will be reserved, cautious, down-to-earth. Somewhat fixed and stubborn in habits. A reliable and productive worker, with powers of endurance. Specially interested in establishing a secure basis for communication of self within his immediate environment.

Moon in:

Aries (☽ ♈): quick-reacting, enthusiastic, excitable; or, impatient, restless, irritable, brusque.

Taurus (☽ ♉): slow-reacting, reserved, cautious, sympathetic; or, unresponsive, fixed habits, stubborn.

Gemini (☽ ♊): unpredictably changeable, quickly adaptive; or, dual-natured, worrisome, inconsistent.

Cancer (☽ ♋): keenly-receptive, sensitive, domesticated; or, clannish, moody, unstable, emotional.

Leo (☽ ♌): cheerful, self-confident, impressive; or, snobbish, self-satisfied, ostentatious.

Virgo (☽ ♍): reserved, modest, meticulous; or, fastidious, timid, nervous.

Libra (☽ ♎): diplomatic, compromising, courteous; or, capricious, evasive, fickle.

Scorpio (☽ ♏): emotionally-charged, reserved, deep; or, resentful, possessive, moody.

Sagittarius (☽ ♐): sincere, cheerful, optimistic, alert; or, offhand manner, careless, restless.

Capricorn (☽ ♑): prudent, cautious, reserved, respectable; or, pessimistic, suspicious, discontented, apprehensive.

Aquarius (☽ ♒): detached, courteous, imaginative, dispassionate; or, unpredictable, erratic, aloof.

Pisces (☽ ♓): kindly, receptive, psychic, amiable; or, touchy, restless, lazy, shy.

MERCURY

Principle: communication.

By Sign: shows mental ability and expressiveness, type of nervous reactions, adaptability to changes, mode of intellectual-intuitive development.

By House: emphasises the sphere of experience through which important *communicative* activities should be developed, and necessary *changes* occur.

Keywords Example: Mercury in Cancer in 5th house.

The *communicative* principle through mental and nervous co-ordination and transmission will function *defensively, sensitively,* focusing on *re-creation and exposition of self.*

Suggested Interpretation: A sensitive, impressionable person, with shrewd, imaginative, intuitive mental faculties. Self-expression will be particularly developed, and the need for an impressive display of the self exercised, through creative, speculative, pleasure-seeking and sporting activities. Frustration could produce touchy and irrational moods.

Mercury in:

Aries (☿ ♈): quick-thinking, frank, witty, self-assertive; or, nervously-restless, sarcastic, quarrelsome, thoughtless.

Taurus (☿ ♉): sensible, thorough, realistic, deliberate; or, slow-thinking, stodgy, prejudiced, brooding.

Gemini (☿ ♊): fluent, clever, alert, inquisitive; or, nervously excitable, imitative, gossipy.

Cancer (☿ ♋): imaginative, intuitive, impressionable, good memory; or, irrational, capricious, narrow-minded.

Leo (☿ ♌): broad-minded, outspoken, optimistic, creative; or, prejudiced, conceited, rude, dogmatic.

Virgo (☿ ♍): analytical, shrewd, discerning, assimilative; or, hyper-critical, worrisome, sarcastic.

Libra (☿ ♎): reasoning, intelligent, balanced, scholarly; or, indecisive, weak-willed, tactless.

Scorpio (☿ ♏): subtle, perceptive, penetrating thought, intuitive; or, sarcastic, suspicious, piercingly critical.

Sagittarius (☿ ♐): frank, versatile, foresighted, open-minded; or, nervous, unstable, dishonest, unconcentrated.

Capricorn (☿ ♑): rational, serious, deliberate; or, censorious, procrastinating, narrow-minded, exacting.

Aquarius (☿ ♒): original, inventive, inquisitive; or, eccentric, abrupt, contrary.

Pisces (☿ ♓): impressionable, intuitive, creative imagination; or, irrational, indecisive, gullible, absent-minded.

VENUS

Principle: unity.

By Sign: shows the quality and intensity of the feelings and affections, sense of personal values, ability to form intimate relationships.

By House: emphasises the sphere of experience through which important *intimate relationships* could be formed, and one's sense of *personal values* be developed.

Keywords Example: Venus in Pisces in 7th house.

The *uniting* principle through sympathy, evaluation, feeling will function *nebulously, impressionably,* focusing on *identification and unity of self with others at personal level.*

Suggested Interpretation: A person of easy-going, sensitive and artistic disposition, who will be strongly attracted to the formation of intimate relationships. A practical approach to marriage should be developed, since there could be a tendency to be too submissive and romantic.

Venus in:

Aries (♀ ♈): ardent, demonstrative, persuasive, popular; or, erotic, self-seeking, self-centred.

Taurus (♀ ♉): affectionate, artistic, sociable, pleasure-loving; or, possessive, grasping, indolent.

Gemini (♀ ♊): coolly-affectionate, light-hearted, good-humoured; or, flirtatious, fickle.

Cancer (♀ ♋): loyal, romantic, tender, sympathetic; or, shy, timid, easily-flattered, possessive.

Leo (♀ ♌): warm-hearted, sincere, creative, artistic; or, patronising, too proud, jealous.

Virgo (♀ ♍): refined, modest, neat, cool; or, fussy, shy, perfectionist.

Libra (♀ ♎): charming, companionable, gentle, loveable; or, frivolous, discontented, untidy, sentimental.

Scorpio (♀ ♏): deep feelings, magnetic charm; or, jealous, hurtful, hateful, immoral.

Sagittarius (♀ ♐): ardent feelings, idealistic, demonstrative; or, inconsiderate, flirtatious, licentious behaviour.

Capricorn (♀ ♑): coolly-affectionate, modest, faithful; or, unfeeling, stern, spiteful, indifferent.

Aquarius (♀ ♒): coolly-affectionate, friendly, quiet, idealistic; or, touchy, uncompromising, unconventional desires.

Pisces (♀ ♓): easy-going, submissive, artistic, sensitive; or, too soft, confused, sloppily sentimental.

MARS

Principle: activity.

By Sign: shows the strength and quality of energetic, passionate and emotional expression, sexual inclinations.

By House: emphasises the sphere of experience through which one's *physical strength, initiative and combative ability* will be challenged.

Keywords Example: Mars in Capricorn in 10th house.

The principle of *activity* through enterprise, self-assertion, energetic expression will function *rationally, prudently*, focusing on *social status, in terms of material responsibilities and necessity.*

Suggested Interpretation: A self-reliant, ambitious and practical person, well-equipped temperamentally to cope with the demands and responsibilities of business life. Success in endeavours through planned economy and industrious effort, prudent control of energy and emotion. Negative tendency could be to selfishly or maliciously achieve ambitions at any cost.

Mars in:

Aries (♂ ♈): impulsive, energetic, passionate, self-willed; or, quick-tempered, aggressive, violent, reckless.

Taurus ($\male$ $\taurus$): industrious, tenacious, practical, purposeful; or, sensuous, extremely obstinate, violent.

Gemini ($\male$ $\gemini$): lively, agile, mechanically-minded; or, highly-strung, argumentative, dissipates energies.

Cancer ($\male$ $\cancer$): sensuous, tenacious, ambitious; or, highly-emotional, irritable, quarrelsome.

Leo ($\male$ $\leo$): dramatic, enthusiastic, ambitious, passionate; or, dominating, arrogant, melodramatic.

Virgo ($\male$ $\virgo$): practical, industrious, ingenious; or, interfering, emotionally frustrated.

Libra ($\male$ $\libra$): ardent affections, persuasive; or, disputatious, vulgar.

Scorpio ($\male$ $\scorpio$): passionate, courageous, strongly-sexed; or, revengeful, brutal, aggressive, sensuous.

Sagittarius ($\male$ $\sagittarius$): sportive, explorative, spirited, independent; or, extremist, uncontrolled, boisterous, rude.

Capricorn ($\male$ $\capricorn$): ambitious, industrious, self-reliant, authoritative; or, irritable, disagreeable, malicious, restless.

Aquarius ($\male$ $\aquarius$): independent, progressive, resolute, enterprising; or, perverse, rebellious, impatient.

Pisces ($\male$ $\pisces$): intensely emotional, generous, temperamental; or, overgushing, sensuous, unstable.

JUPITER

Principle: expansion.

By Sign: shows characteristic ability to seize opportunities for expansion through growth, materially and by understanding.

By House: emphasises the sphere of experience through which opportunities for *material expansion or growth of consciousness*, and *compensation for life's disappointments*, can be found.

Keywords Example: Jupiter in Scorpio in 6th house.

The principle of *expansion* through growth, materially and by understanding, will function *penetratingly*, *intensely*, focusing on *conformity and service to the community*, *conditioned by health and efficiency*.

Suggested Interpretation: A proud, ambitious person, of keen judgment, shrewd and penetrating understanding. Intensity of purpose can achieve the efficiency his principles demand in his work within the pattern of the community, and in maintenance of a healthy, wholesome mind and body. Negative tendency could produce conceit, self-indulgent habits.

Jupiter in:

Aries (♃ ♈): self-sufficient, generous, freedom-loving, high-spirited; or, extravagant, boastful, bullying, over-optimistic.

Taurus (♃ ♉): sound judgment, good-hearted, reliable; or, self-indulgent, self-opinionated, exploitative.

Gemini (♃ ♊): highly intelligent, varied talents, broad-minded; or, crafty, diffuse and scattered interests, indiscreet.

Cancer (♃ ♋): kindly, protective, charitable; or, extremely touchy, too conscientious.

Leo (♃ ♌): generous, big-hearted, dignified; or, over-bearing, intolerant, self-appraising, extravagant.

Virgo (♃ ♍): conscientious, intellectual; or, haughty, cynical.

Libra (♃ ♎): sympathetic, just, charitable, hospitable; or, conceited, lazy.

Scorpio (♃ ♏): shrewd, keen judgment, ambitious, proud; or, aggressive, conceited, self-indulgent.

Sagittarius (♃ ♐): optimistic, philosophical, jovial, liberal-minded; or, extravagant, boastful, lawless.

Capricorn (♃ ♑): resourceful, responsible, productive, conscientious; or, mean, bigoted, austere, self-righteous.

Aquarius (♃ ♒): broad-minded, humanitarian, philosophical, impartiality; or, rudely tactless, intolerant.

Pisces (♃ ♓): compassionate, benevolent, genial, humorous; or, extravagant, unreliable, over-imaginative.

SATURN

Principle: formative.

By Sign: shows characteristic ability for self-discipline, sense of personal inadequacy and limitation, quality of self-consciousness.

By House: emphasises the sphere of experience through which *personal limitation, frustration and suffering* can be felt most.

Keywords Example: Saturn in Aries in 4th house.

The *formative* principle through restriction, discipline, rigidity will function *objectively*, *urgently*, focusing on *self, possessions, and intimate relatives as a basis for new growth.*

Suggested Interpretation: A self-reliant, active, ambitious person, persevering and calculating with plans for achieving objectives, yet always ready for the right opportunities. Family responsibilities, a fear of insecurity in home matters, could limit success in business. Negative tendency could produce destructiveness, cruelty, an autocratic attitude.

Saturn in:

Aries (♄ ♈): ambitious, persistent, self-reliant, mechanical ingenuity; or, autocratic, irresponsible, destructive, cruel.

Taurus (♄ ♉): stable, methodical, endurance, constructiveness; or, materialistic, dour, avaricious.

Gemini (♄ ♊): intellectual, scientific, calculating, impartial; or, sceptical, critical, inhibited expression.

Cancer (♄ ♋): ambitious, shrewd, self-centred; or, suspicious, miserly, self-pitying, too-defensive.

Leo (♄ ♌): authoritative, self-assured, responsible; or, resentful of limitations.

Virgo (♄ ♍): methodical, precise, practical, prudent; or, pedantic, hypercritical, mistrustful, exacting.

Libra (♄ ♎): tactful, particular, impartial; or, insincere, impractical, austere.

Scorpio (♄ ♏): purposeful, strong reserve, secretive; or, cruel, brooding, sceptical, selfish.

Sagittarius (♄ ♐): moralising, ambitious, trustworthy, dignified; or, tactless, insincere.

Capricorn (♄ ♑): methodical, patient, disciplined, dutiful; or, pessimistic, hard, selfish, melancholic.

Aquarius (♄ ♒): studious, sincere, scientific; or, dogmatic, cunning.

Pisces (♄ ♓): self-sacrificing, retiring; or, self-pitying, untidy, worrisome.

Important note: Uranus, Neptune and Pluto BY SIGN show the formation of general, impersonal characteristics typical of a whole generation, because they take about 7, 14 and 20 years respectively to transit a sign (see pages 29 and 32). Even when one of these three planets can be considered as a personal or unique factor, the *function* of the planet should be emphasised in interpretation, in preference to the characteristics of the *sign* being stressed by the planet's presence therein. Say, for example, Uranus in Leo is square Sun in Taurus. You would refer to the suggested interpretation for Sun-sq-Uranus, also that for an afflicted Sun in Taurus, and blend these in your own way. You need not bother to interpret Uranus in Leo. Another example, Uranus conjunction Leo Ascendant. You will refer to the suggested interpretation for Uranus-conj-Ascendant, and for a Leo Ascendant (the characteristics for Leo, Chapter 4), and blend these.

In short, your interpretation of Uranus, irrespective of the sign it is in, will be the same, because it is the principle of Uranus which will be more evident in the personal make-up than its expression through the sign. The same applies to Neptune and Pluto. This is not implying that these planets will not emphasise the characteristics of a sign they are in, but the significance will be so subtly a part of the mode of behaviour the individual adopts *collectively* with the millions of others of his own generation, that they are best ignored in a personal interpretation. When you are more experienced at interpretation you may have developed your own ideas about what I have just said, but at present I would suggest you follow my advice, to avoid the fault that so many make: over-emphasis of the signs containing these three extra-Saturnian planets.

Uranus, Neptune and Pluto by house

Uranus: emphasises the sphere of experience through which one should seek *freedom and originality* of expression, and through which *unconventional* experiences and *drastic changes* may be expected.

Neptune: emphasises the sphere of experience through which one could be attracted to *mystical and religious ideals*, and encounter *peculiar, mysterious or chaotic* developments.

Pluto: emphasises the sphere of experience through which critical *transformations* could occur, resulting in *explosive endings and beginnings* to distinct phases of life development.

12

Preparing for interpretation

There are no set rules for classifying the various factors in a birth-chart prior to the actual interpretation.

It is best that the beginner takes the trouble to set down preliminary notes about a chart he wants to interpret, and follows some kind of method for classifying these deductions. In this way he will get a clear grasp of the chart-pattern, be less likely to overlook important features, and learn to do the job properly and not treat the whole thing as though it were just a parlour game. Students taking the Courses in astrology with the Mayo School of Astrology are taught to set out their preliminary deductions to a definite, detailed method. Once they know what they are doing and have completed the Courses they can naturally devise their own method of assessing a chart if they wish. You can do the same. But, first, you have to learn how you should classify the most important factors in a chart.

Each factor in the chart (planet, sign, aspect, etc.) has its own relative importance to the whole pattern, but the three factors that are always considered of prime importance are the *Ascendant*, *Sun* and *Moon*. In my opinion in that order. In fact, a very true assessment of an individual's character can be made from those three factors alone – judged from the signs they are associated with and houses and aspects involved, or even just by signs.

However, the first notes you must make will concern the following classifications which must be given special consideration in the final assessment of character and life-pattern:

(1) Ascendant by sign.
(2) Ascendant-Ruler by sign and house position.
(3) Sun by sign and house position.
(4) Moon by sign and house position.

(5) Angular planets.
(6) Positive and Negative.
(7) Triplicities (Elements).
(8) Quadruplicities (Qualities).
(9) Main aspect-patterns.

Then you will make notes regarding each planet by sign, aspects and house position. From these notes you will construct your final analysis.

Preliminary notes for Linda's chart

So that you clearly understand the procedure we will make notes on the example chart that we have already calculated. We begin with the classifications of the 9 most important features.

(1) *Ascendant:* Pisces (♓).
(2) *Ascendant co-Rulers:* Neptune in Virgo (♆ ♍) in 7th; Jupiter in Cancer (♃ ♋) in 5th.
(3) *Sun* in Cancer (☉ ♋) in 5th.
(4) *Moon* in Pisces (☽ ♓) in 1st.
(5) *Angular planets* (i.e., within 8° orb of conjunction Asc., Desc., M.C. or I.C.): Mercury in Gemini (☿ ♊).
(6) *Positive and Negative* (total planets, Sun to Saturn only, and Asc., M.C., in either Positive or Negative signs):
  Positive: 5
  Negative: 4
(7) *Triplicities* (Elements) (planets as with Positive and Negative):
  Fire: 2 (M.C., ♂)
  Earth: 0
  Air: 3 (☿ ♀ ♄)
  Water: 4 (Asc., ☉ ☽ ♃)
(8) *Quadruplicities* (Qualities) (planets as with Positive and Negative):
  Cardinal: 2 (☉ ♃)
  Fixed: 1 (♂)
  Mutable: 6 (Asc., M.C., ☽ ☿ ♀ ♄)
(9) *Main aspect-patterns:* T-Sq. in Mutable signs (☿ □ (☽ ☍ ♆)); feeling-uniting/formative/deviational emphasis (♀ ☌ ♄ ☌ ♅); self-integration/expansion emphasis (☉ ☌ ♃).

This person will not be thought of astrologically as a *Cancerian*, because they have 'Sun in Cancer'. The Ascendant is the more personal feature, therefore they will be *Piscean, of Cancerian group-type.*
Your deductions, in note form, of what is meant by each planet by

sign and house and aspects, will be taken from the chapters dealing with these. In the following deductions *minor aspects* have been omitted so that you may more clearly recognise the essential features.

General features (example chart):

Significator	Deduction
♌ ☋ (7th-1st)	Benefits will be received through partnerships and intimate associates with whom you share yourself on equal terms; sacrifice of self-centred interests.
4 Water, 0 Earth	Emotional and intuitive features will be pronounced, but a lack of the practical, down-to-earth, stabilising and restraining element.
6 Mutable	Extremely adaptable, changeable, restless; lack of concentration.
1 Fixed	
T-Sq. (☿ □ (☽ ☍ ♆)), ☿ at apex, or focus on 4th house	Major problems could develop through self-centred interests, intimate relationships or partnerships, conflicting with home/family interests.

Ascendant Pisces

♓	Impressionable, passive, emotional, adaptable, restless personality. Compassionate, kindly, sympathetic, very easy-going. Intensely emotional and submissive when in love. Creative, psychic. *Faults:* impractical, over-emotional, indecisive. *Career:* artistic expression, social worker. *Psychological:* urge to transcend the material; simplicity of being. *Health:* weak feet, abdominal, intestinal, nerves.
Asc. □ ♀ ♄ ♅	Emotional frustration/disappointment could upset health; unconventional.
Asc. △ . ♃	Cheerful, optimistic personality-attitude.

Ascendant co-Rulers

Neptune in 7th	*Keywords: Refining* principle through dissolution, subtlety, immateriality will focus on *identification and unity of self with others at per-*

sonal level. Peculiar, mysterious or chaotic experiences through intimate relationships/ partnerships.

Ψ P and ☍ ☽   Refined, subtle response; extreme emotional sensitivity and instability; psychic, artistic; possible deceitfulness, self-deception, escapist tendencies.

Ψ □ ☿   Subtlety, sensitivity of mental expression, easily disturbed nervous system; idealistic, impressionable; confused thinking, absent-mindedness, vague fears and imaginings.

Ψ □ ♃   Self-expansion through refined, creative, intuitive perceptiveness; response to devotional, mystical, artistic, philosophical impulses; tendency to escapist, emotionally-charged, sensation-seeking compensations for personal inadequacies.

Ψ □ M.C.   Sensitive, artistic, out-of-the-ordinary Ego-complex; nervous-emotional tension.

Ψ △ ♅   Successful imaginative, creative, unconventional expression.

Jupiter in ♋ in 5th   *Keywords:* Principle of *expansion* through growth, materially and by understanding will function *defensively, sensitively,* focusing on *re-creation and exposition of self.*

♃ ♋   Kindly, protective, charitable; possible touchiness.

♃ in 5th   Growth of understanding, and compensation for dissappointments, inhibitions, through creative, self-exhibitive expression, pleasures, taking risks, love-making.

♃ P and ☌ ☉   Powerful self-expansive impulses; optimistic, good-humoured, generous, just, harmonious patterns of behaviour; conscientious, opportunist.

♃ △ Asc., □ Ψ   (See Asc. Ψ).

♃ P ♇   Self-expansion through ability to make new beginnings from existing 'worn out' conditions, though risk of drastic forms of compensation for personal inadequacies.

Sun

☉ ♋ in 5th

Keywords: Principle of *self-integration* will function *defensively, sensitively,* focusing on *recreation and exposition of self.*

☉ ♋

Shrewd, resourceful, sensitive, protective; possible touchiness, self-pity, over-emotionalism.

☉ in 5th

Necessary experiences for self-integration, growth of character, through organising of qualities into impressive, creative, powerful projection of self; pleasures, sports, love-making, children.

☉ △ Asc., ☌ P ♃

(See Asc. ♃).

☉ P ♇

Powerful transforming, regenerative impulses; deep-rooted unconscious drives could compel elimination of obstructing psychological features at critical stages in life.

Sun-Ruler: Moon

☽ ♓ in 1st

Keywords: Principle of *rhythms* through instinctive response, assimilation, reflection will function *nebulously, impressionably,* focusing on *self-centred interests.*

☽ ♓

Kindly, receptive, psychic, amiable; need to avoid being touchy, restless, lazy, shy.

☽ in 1st

Will respond to situations for furthering self-centred interests that could bring major changes.

☽ □ ☿

Quick nervous and mental response, sensitivity, possible indecision, worry, restlessness.

☽ □ M.C.

Responsive Ego-complex, sensitive; emotional discord.

☽ P and ☍ Ψ

(See Ψ).

Mercury

☿ ♊ in 4th

Keywords: Communicative principle through mental and nervous co-ordination and transmission will function *adaptively, variably,* focusing on *self, possessions, intimate relatives as a basis for new growth.*

☿ ♊	Fluent, clever, alert, inquisitive mental attributes; nervously excitable, imitative.
☿ in 4th	Important communicative activities developed and necessary changes likely through home and family experiences, parental influence.
☿ □ ☽ ♆	(See ☽ ♆).
☿ P ♀	Mental and nervous activity stimulated by feelings; charm, gentleness, agreeable disposition.
☿ P ♂	Quick mental/nervous reactions; forthright, enterprising, incisive; tendency to overstrain, recklessness.
☿ P ♄	Capacity for disciplined mental expression, coolly regulated nervous reactions; profound, logical thinking; lack of confidence, depressiveness, apprehension.
☿ P ♅	Originality, high-strung nervous system, inventive, dramatic; possible extremist ideas.
☿ ☍ M.C.	Mentally/nervously active Ego-complex; underlying disharmony, excitability.

Venus

♀ ♊ in 4th	*Keywords: Uniting* principle through sympathy, evaluation, feeling, will function *adaptively, variably,* focusing on *self, possessions and intimate relatives as a basis for new growth.*
♀ ♊	Coolly-affectionate, light-hearted, good-humoured; possible weakness: flirtatious, fickle.
♀ in 4th	Important relationships formed, personal values developed, through home/family experiences, parental influence.
♀ P ☿	(See ☿).
♀ P and ♂ ♄	Limited or disciplined feelings; disappointments in love, delayed marriage; strict values, faithful; tendency to selfish and exacting feelings, sense of loneliness.
♀ P and ♂ ♅	Abnormal or very excitable feelings, unusual tastes, unconventional values, artistic talent, magnetic charm; independent, romantic; tendency to illicit or broken love affairs, separations.

♀ □ Asc.	(See Asc.).
♀ P and ✳ ♂	Passionate feelings and sensual nature; quickly forms ties of affection; demonstrative; strong sex nature.
♀ ✳ ♇	Ability to eliminate, release undesired/disturbing feelings.

Mars

♂ ♌ in 6th	Principle of *activity* through enterprise, self-assertion, energetic expression will function *powerfully, impressively*, focusing on *conformity and service to the community, conditioned by health and efficiency.*
♂ ♌	Dramatic, enthusiastic, ambitious, passionate; possible faults: dominating, melodramatic.
♂ in 6th	Initiative, combative ability, challenged through need to conform to a disciplined and active pattern of behaviour and service within the community. Health could be undermined by strenuous exertion, over-stress, emotion.
♂ P ☿, P ✳ ♀	(See ☿ ♀).
♂ P and ✳ ♄	Self-assertive, disciplined, formative impulses.
♂ ☌ ♇	A need to transform excess emotional/passional energies into constructive expression, to avoid explosive temper.
♂ △ M.C.	Assertive, energetic, emotionally-inclined Ego-complex.

Saturn

♄ ♊ in 4th	*Formative* principle through restriction, discipline, rigidity will function *adaptively, variably,* focusing on *self, possessions and intimate relatives as a basis for new growth.*
♄ ♊	Intellectual, calculating; possible weakness: inhibited expression.
♄ in 4th	Personal limitation, frustration, suffering could be most felt through home/family experiences, parental influence.
♄ ☌ P ♀, P ☿, □ Asc., ✳ P ♂	(See Asc. ☿ ♀ ♂).

♄ P and ♂ ♅	Determined self-will; alternating depressive, nervously-tensed moods.
♄ ✳ ♙	Ability to control and sensibly reject disturbing thoughts caused by frustration.

Uranus

♅ in 3rd	Principle of *deviation* through invention, independence, drastic change, will focus on *relationship of self to environment*.
	Freedom, originality of expression will be developed, and unconventional incidents and drastic changes occur, through experiences involving brothers and sisters, casual acquaintances, short journeys, desire to relate and communicate self directly to immediate environment.
♅ ✳ ♙	Deep-rooted tendency to dynamic creative expression.

(For other Uranus aspects see: Asc. ☿ ♀ ♄ ♆).

Pluto

♙ in 5th	*Transforming* principle through elimination, renewal, will focus on *recreation and exposition of self*.
	Critical transformations could occur, resulting in explosive endings and beginnings to distinct phases of life development, through experiences relating to creative, self-exhibitive expression, and pleasure, love-making, children.

(For other Pluto aspects see Asc. ⊙ ♀ ♂ ♃ ♄ ♅).

M.C. ♐	Conscious of yourself as needing to be free-ranging, optimistic, frank, versatile, philosophical; tendency for exaggeration, extremism, restlessness.

(For M.C. aspects see ☽ ☿ ♂ ♆).

13

Interpreting the chart

Now that you have made classified notes on Linda's chart, how should you begin to put these together correctly? The best plan is to divide your analysis into the following sections:

(Planets referred to are to be interpreted *by sign and aspects;* houses, *by cusp-sign and planets therein.*)

1. *General Characteristics:* primarily Sun and Moon; Sun-Ruler, Moon-Ruler; any outstanding feature or aspect-pattern.

2. *Personality-Attitude:* primarily Ascendant; Ascendant-Ruler; any planet in Ascending sign; any planet aspecting Ascendant.

3. *Mentality:* Mercury; Mercury-Ruler; Jupiter and Saturn (deeper growth-patterns of mental development); M.C., M.C.-Ruler (the Ego); 3rd house (casual, conversational mode of mental communicativeness); 9th (more profound, philosophical, academical, 'higher consciousness' qualities).

4. *Emotional Nature, Personal Contact:* Venus (feelings, affections, ability to attract others); Mars (emotions, sex, conflict with others); Water signs (emotional strength); Moon (emotional and sensation response); 1st (attitude towards using others for mainly self-centred interests); 3rd (brothers, sisters, neighbours, casual acquaintances); 4th (parental influence); 5th (love affairs, children); 7th (marriage, partnerships); 8th (sexual love); 9th (in-laws); 11th (friendships without need for personal ties).

5. *Business, Financial Interests, Career:* 10th (urge and ability to develop a career, general business prospects); 2nd (resourcefulness, earning ability); 5th (speculative prospects); 6th (working ability, employees); 7th (business partners); 8th (material benefits through others); Jupiter (ability to develop material assets and seize opportunities for expan-

sion); Saturn (ability to plan, conserve, discipline, endure); Mars (initiative, enterprise).

6. *Travel:* 3rd (short journeys); 9th (long journeys, overseas); Mercury, Jupiter (urge to travel).

7. *Health:* Ascendant, afflicted Sun or Moon, Saturn, 6th (physical weakness); 12th (chronic illness or severely undermining psychological conflict); any other severely afflicted planet.

In your first attempts at calculating and interpreting a chart on your own you will naturally begin with people you know. Try first with people whose time of birth is known (within half an hour if possible). In these cases you will have the all-important Ascendant and M.C., also the house positions of planets, to work on.

The serious astrological-consultant will not attempt 'guess work' for clients: he insists that he is given a few details concerning the general status of his client. In this way the full value of the chart-pattern as a guide to character potentialities and future prospects is realised in the light of existing personal circumstances and problems. After all, a dustman and a king could both be born at the same time in the same city, but though character-potentialities and the favourable or unfavourable trends throughout life would be identical, their circumstances of birth would provide totally contrasting opportunities for unfoldment.

I will not interpret in detail our example chart from the notes made in the previous chapter. Instead, I will make a few helpful observations on this case.

It is the chart of a young lady, Linda, who has kindly given permission for her case to be used.

The chart-pattern clearly indicates her essential nature. She is easygoing, extremely emotional, sensitive, impressionable (Asc. ☽ in ♓; ☉ ♃ in ♋). She admits to being touchy, untidy, at times careless and impractical. She consulted me at a time when a dramatic and entirely new chapter had begun in her life. It was late 1960. She was then 18, and had a 2-month-old illegitimate child. The dramatic disruption of her life was clearly indicated by the astrological pattern forming in her life at that time, as you will be shown in the next chapter (Progressions and Transits). She had reached a period in her life when the Uranus and Pluto principles coincided with major developments, both signifying disruptive events, new, unplanned, drastic changes. There was an emphasis at that time on emotional factors, and so this trend, which could have unfolded in countless different ways, involved her in an unfortunate emotional experience. Her life-pattern was certainly *transformed*, and as Pluto at her birth had indicated it would occur – in a 5th house manner!

Remember the notes we have made concerning this girl's proneness to deception through the emotions (Asc. ♓, ☽ ☍ ♆, ☿ □ ☽ ♆, ♆ afflicted in 7th house); the likelihood of disappointments in love (♀ ☌ ♄); her attraction to unconventional sexual experience (♀ ☌ ♅); the submissive, easily stimulated emotional nature (Asc. ☽ in ♓, ☉ ☌ ♃ in ♋); and the focus of the expansive, generous-natured ☉ ☌ ♃ factor in the 5th house sphere of life (love-making, children).

Due to sensitivity and shyness (♓ ♋) and inhibiting parental influence (♀ ☌ ♄ 4th) she had never had a boy friend on sweetheart terms prior to this affair. In all sincerity she told me she held no bitterness against the father, even though he had apparently 'vanished over the horizon' shortly after she told him she was carrying his child. Her parents, deeply shocked, persuaded her to have the child away from their hometown, and to get it adopted, which it now is.

The factors I have just referred to in Linda's chart indicate her vulnerability through the emotions, and her so easily submissive response to kindness and sympathy shown by others. That so early in life she allowed herself to be deceived, or perhaps was too generous with her affections, and unfortunate with the consequences, does not mean fatalistically that she will always be unfortunate in her 'love life'. I stressed to her the vulnerability of her nature, which she admitted was true, and with this knowledge of a very weak link in her make-up she is forearmed for the future and can endeavour to strengthen herself in this respect so that she does not experience a similar emotional upset.

As would be expected from her chart, Linda has artistic and creative talent, and is training in her spare time to be a commercial artist. She is from a middle-class family, and though she has had no special education she definitely has above-average intelligence, and a shrewd, assimilative mind. The adaptability and versatility (♓ ♊) became evident when she related the 11 different jobs, from dressmaking to shorthand-typist, she had had in less than 3 years! It was not just that she would become restless and seek a change, but also her ability to interest herself in a variety of subjects caused her to vary her work. The afflictions involving ☽ ☿ ♃ with ♆, which is not helped one bit by the Pisces Ascendant, point to the underlying impractical nature, confused idealism, and tendency to dissipate the energies and talents with the risk of becoming a 'Jack of all trades and master of none'.

Through this chart we see a sensitive, unassertive, easy-going personality (Asc. ♓). The intelligently adaptable mental-nervous reactions provide an ideal channel for her versatile, charming, imaginative and original self-expression (☿ ♊, ☿-♀ ♅). She can discipline herself to cool, calculating thoughts (☿ P ♄), and react in a persuasive, forthright manner to situations (☿ P ♂). But essentially her self-expression will be coloured and stimulated by the restless, powerful emotional energies, her intuitive and impressionable mind, her capacity for intense feeling reaction to life and people (Asc. ♓, strong Water/Mutable signs, ☉ ♃ ♋, ☿ □ ☽ ♆). Major trends in her life will be determined by personal contacts, out-of-the-ordinary experiences, rather than career and business developments. There is too much restlessness likely to pitch her into insecure, chaotic, disillusioning circumstances, for there to be a distinct rhythm and harmony to her psychological development.

She will need to guard against escapist impulses (♆-☿ ☽) when under emotional and nervous strain and excitement. Fortunately she is fully aware of the need for optimism, good humour, and a philosophical attitude (M.C. ♐, ☉ ☌ ♃), and she will undoubtedly learn what assets these qualities can be. Her personal happiness and material success in life will depend very much on the instinctive manner in which she integrates and organises her faculties and talents, indicated by ☉ ☌ ♃ in ♋. This will require the positive, expansive expression of her emotional, sensitive, intuitive faculties, rather than a primarily rational and reasoned understanding of herself and experiences. Any ill-health will most likely be the result of mental, nervous and emotional tension and over-excitement. There will be a tendency to bronchial trouble (♄ ☿ afflicted in ♊); nervously aggravated digestive and abdominal disorders, possible feet complaints (Asc. ☽ in ♓, ☉ ♃ ♋).

14

Progressions and transits

Progressions. *Progressions* are the calculations by which the life-pattern, the probable trends of circumstances, for any year past, present or future, can be determined. Astrologers have devised numerous methods for 'progressing the natal chart'. You will be taught what is known as the 'day for a year' method. All progressions, whatever the method, stem from the natal chart calculated for the moment of birth, and can be thought of as extended calculations to the natal chart.

A day for a year. Like all methods of progressions this method is of a *symbolic* nature. This is because each day after the day of one's birth symbolically represents a whole year of one's life. We don't know why this is, yet it is so. Put in another way, the Earth rotates on its axis in 24 hours, one astronomical day. The relative movements of the planets to the birth-chart during those 24 hours correspond to the way one can expect one's life to map out during one whole year, when interpreted astrologically. Even the Bible mentions this method for prophesying: 'I have appointed thee each day for a year.' (Ezekiel: 4: 6.)

The G.M.T. date of birth for our example chart is 3rd July 1942. For calculating progressions the *Ephemeris* for the year of birth is used. Thus, if we wanted to know the significant trends of circumstances, and the nature of opportunities presented for character growth and material benefit, for Linda during her 16th year, we would count forward 16 days from her date of birth. 3rd July +16 days = 19th July. The planets will have progressed forward (or backward if retrograde) from their positions in the natal chart to their positions in longitude and declination shown for the 19th July.

Now the important thing about the progressed planets is whether they form aspects with each other (progressed planet to progressed planet), or to any of the planets, Ascendant or M.C. in the natal chart (progressed to natal). It is these aspects that indicate to us the probable trends in the life during the particular year.

Perpetual Noon-Date. Turn to the July pages from *Raphael's 1942 Ephemeris*. Against the 24th July is written *1963*, because the positions of the planets by progression correspond to *1963* for our example chart. Linda will be 21 in 1963: 3rd July+21=24th July (day for a year method).

If we calculate the planets' positions for 10.34 p.m. (G.M.T.) (Linda's birth-time), 24th July 1942, for Windsor, these would be their progressed positions corresponding to 3rd July 1963. But this would be a laborious process. Every year for which we want to find the progressed aspects operative, we must do all those calculations as for the natal chart.

But we don't need to. All we have to do is find the *Perpetual Noon-Date*. This date will correspond to the noon positions of the planets in the *Ephemeris*, and without doing any calculations we simply copy down the noon positions of the planets for the year in question.

To Find the Perpetual Noon-Date. Each day consists of 24 hours, which correspond to 1 year or 12 months. Thus:

$$24 \text{ hours} = 12 \text{ months}$$
$$6 \text{ hours} = 3 \text{ months}$$
$$2 \text{ hours} = 1 \text{ month}$$

1 hour	=	0 month	15 days (approx.)
$\frac{1}{2}$ hour	=	0 month	$7\frac{1}{2}$ days (,,)
5 minutes	=	0 month	$1\frac{1}{4}$ days (,,)
1 minute	=	0 month	$\frac{1}{4}$ day (,,)

Linda's birth-time was 10.34 p.m. (G.M.T.), i.e., 10 hours 34 minutes *after* noon. Using the above table:

10 hours	= 5 months
30 minutes	= 0 month $7\frac{1}{2}$ days (approx.)
4 minutes	= 0 month 1 day (,,)

10 hours 34 minutes = 5 months $8\frac{1}{2}$ days (say 9 days)

When birth is p.m. we *subtract* the total (equivalent months and days to the interval from noon to birth) from the birth *date*. When birth is a.m. we *add* the total (equivalent months and days to the interval from birth to noon) to the birth *date*.

Linda's birth date	= 3rd July
subtract	5m. 9d.

Perpetual Noon-Date = 25th Jan. (approx.)

The Perpetual Noon-Date of 25th January, calculated proportionately, is accurate to within a day or so, which is perfectly good for all practical purposes. Therefore:

> Noon 3rd July 1942 corresponds to 25th January 1942
> Noon 4th July 1942   „   „ 25th January 1943
> Noon 5th July 1942   „   „ 25th January 1944

And so on. If we count forward 21 days from Linda's birth date, 3rd July, we come to 24th July. Noon positions of the planets on 24th July are their progressed longitudes and declinations corresponding to 25th January 1963.

You have to think now in terms of 1 day equalling 1 year. The distance travelled in longitude by a planet in 1 day as shown in the *Ephemeris* is its distance covered by progression in 12 months. Every planet except the Moon travels a relatively short distance. With the Moon travelling about 1° per month we need to calculate its position for each month of the year so that we can accurately list any aspects the Moon forms.

Calculating the Progressed Moon. We want to find the Moon's positions for each month January–December 1963.

> Moon on 25 July (corresponding to 25 January 1964) = ♐ 29° 36′
> Moon on 24 July („   „ 25 January 1963) = ♐ 14° 41′
> ────────
> Moon's motion during year   =   14° 55′

Divide 14° 55′ by 12, gives the average motion each month, which is 1° 14′ and 7′ over.

> Moon's longitude 1963 25 January   = ♐ 14° 41′
>   25 February =   15° 56′
>   25 March   =   17° 10′
>   25 April   =   18° 25′
>   25 May   =   19° 39′
>   25 June   =   20° 54′
>   25 July   =   22° 08′
>   25 August   =   23° 23′
>   25 September =   24° 37′
>   25 October   =   25° 52′
>   25 November =   27° 06′
>   25 December =   28° 21′

Progressed Moon's aspects. In calculating possible aspects formed by progressed planets you follow the same procedure as for aspects between natal planets. The only difference is that you want to know just the *exact* aspects, and when they occur. No orb is allowed. Another point is that I have rarely found minor aspects worth the trouble to calculate. We will only look for major aspects (☌ P ✶ □ △ ☍).

Linda's progressed Moon moved between ♐ 14°–28° during 1963. Refer to her natal chart and see if any major aspects are formed *exactly* with these degrees. Bear in mind that the positions of the progressed Moon we have listed correspond to the 25th day of each month. You should be able to find the following aspects to natal planets:

> May 1963: prog. ☽☌ M.C.
> June   : prog. ☽☍ ☿
> Sept.   : prog. ☽ □ ☽
> Nov.   : prog. ☽ □ Ψ

Now run your finger along the planets' longitudes for 24th July in the *1942 Ephemeris*, corresponding to 25th January 1963, and see if the progressed Moon forms aspects with any progressed planet. You should find the following:

> Oct. 1963: prog. ☽ △ ♂ prog.
> Dec. 1963: prog. ☽ □ Ψ prog.

Until you buy printed forms for progressed data you should make your own, writing the progressed Moon's longitude and aspects against each respective month for 1963.

Progressed Planets' aspects. Although we are primarily concerned with aspects formed by progressed planets during 1963, I always list major progressed and transiting aspects for 2 years prior to the current year and for 5 years ahead. However, we will calculate possible progressed aspects for 1962–65. As already mentioned, we only want to know when aspects occur *exactly*, not necessarily to the actual month as with the Moon, but to the year of exactitude. First, refer the longitude of each progressed planet to the natal chart.

Begin with the Sun. 1962–65 corresponds to 23rd–26th July, and during this period the Sun progressed between ♋ 29° 59' and ♌ 2° 51'. Remember these noon positions are for 25th January, the beginning of each year.

First thing we make a note of is that the Sun changed signs, from ♋ to ♌ in 1962. No aspect during 1963. 1964 Sun~p~ ✶ ♅. No aspect 1965. Next we check for parallel aspects by the progressed Sun. 1962–65 Sun progressed from 20° 9' to 19° 31' in declination. Check with natal

planets' declinations for *exact* parallel aspect. You should find the
following:

1963 ☉ₚ P ♀, P ♄
1964 ☉ₚ P ☿

Proceed in the same way with the other progressed planets. List any
aspects to natal planets against the respective years. I will give the complete list of aspects presently. Next, look for aspects between progressed
planets.

Transits. With the progressions you used the *Ephemeris* for the year
of birth. To find aspects from transiting planets to natal planets you
must use the *Ephemeris* for the year in question. For example, we want
to know any major aspects formed by transiting planets *to natal* planets
during 1963, so we shall have to refer to the *1963 Ephemeris*. For 1964
we refer to the *1964 Ephemeris*. If we want to find possible transiting
aspects that might correspond with an important event in our own life
in 1927, we refer to a *1927 Ephemeris*.

Transits, therefore, are the planets' positions in the current Ephemeris, for whatever year we want to calculate their aspects for.

As with progressions, I generally only list the *major* aspects. Aspects
between two transiting planets are only considered of personal significance
if the degrees the aspect occurs in forms an aspect with planets, Ascendant, or M.C. in an individual's natal chart. Otherwise they are ignored,
and only transiting planets *to the natal chart* are considered. As the *1962–
65 Ephemerides* are not reproduced in this book you cannot check for
transiting aspects relative to our example chart, but I will list these with
the progressed aspects.

Duration of Progressed and Transiting aspects. Both progressed
and transisting aspects are considered effective when within 1° of
exactness, and until 1° past. A duration of 2°. An aspect of the progressed Sun to a natal planet will always last about 2 years, since the
Sun progresses about 1° per year. But an aspect between the Sun and a
progressed planet may last for as much as 30 or more years, if both
bodies are moving at about the same pace. Rarely do the planets from
Jupiter to Pluto form progressed aspects, even to natal planets, since
these move so slowly throughout a lifetime of 70 years even. Thus,
it is the faster-moving progressed planets will form most aspects and
provide more activity and events in the life. Progressed Moon aspects
last about 1 month, and are not to be considered anything like as important as the aspects formed by the other progressed planets.

With transits, aspects formed by ♃ ♄ ♅ ♆ ♇ are of most importance. ☉ ☽ ☿ ♀ ♂ move so much more quickly that the effects of their aspects last only brief periods – with transiting ☽ but a few hours, ☿ when moving at its fastest little more than a day.

Interpreting Progressed and Transiting aspects. *Progressed* aspects appear to correlate primarily with psychological developments from within the individual, often, of course, stimulated by exterior events which also correlate with the nature of the aspect. *Transiting* aspects appear to correlate more often with the development of circumstances in the life, which are invariably outside the individual's power to prevent happening. They *do* sometimes correlate purely with psychological development, though more frequently this is due to exterior happenings which demand particular reactions from the individual or force problems upon him which test his character or ability to cope with them. *No* aspect, however, brings a fate that cannot be counteracted in some way and some benefit derived therefrom, unless it correlates with death!

The most important thing to *always bear in mind* when interpreting these aspects is that the pattern of the natal chart always determines their value. For example, if Sun and Jupiter were in square aspect natally, even a trine aspect from transiting Jupiter to Sun cannot be expected to produce the usual favourable effects, at least, not without some initial problem or difficulty correlative with the Sun–Jupiter affliction at birth. Equally, if Sun was not in aspect with Jupiter at birth, the typically fortunate and expansive conjunction of transiting Jupiter to natal Sun will not have anything like the effect as would be the case were they favourably aspected at birth.

In short, the pattern of the natal chart we carry with us all our life. The progressed and transiting movements of the planets indicate the phases in our lives when the potentialities shown in our natal chart will be given opportunities for development, whether through favourable or apparent unfavourable circumstances. It is unwise to attempt to predict actual events. The nature of the *trends* should only be given, since so many scores of different events could probably correlate with a certain trend of 'planetary influences'.

When interpreting progressed or transiting aspects always base your reasoning on the principles of the planets, signs and houses involved, but *especially* the planets. You must also assess the probable effects, and the likely reaction of the individual concerned, according to the natal chart *as a whole*, and the status and circumstances of the individual.

Transiting Jupiter conjunction the Sun will need a different interpretation when it occurs in the chart of a child of 5, a reigning monarch and a dustman! If you remember it should correlate with a period of expansion, happiness, good favour, you won't go far wrong.

Sun (progressed): A period of major importance. Psychologically, and through correlative circumstances, the time will be ripe for important adjustments, organising and integrating of the whole life pattern, as directed by the planet involved in aspect with the Sun.

Moon (progressed): A period of about 1 month's duration, in which affairs and psychological features associated with the planet aspected will be emphasised, activated.

Mercury (progressed): Usually indicates changes, necessary readjustments, increased mental activity, travel, literary matters of above-average importance.

Venus (progressed): Period of much importance regards emotional, personal, creative interests. Can mean marriage, falling in love – or out of love, inspired creative work, birth of a child, emphasis on money matters.

Mars (progressed, trans.): Period of increased activity, conflict, enterprise. Energy must be controlled, impulsive action avoided. More accident-prone. Can be ideal period for taking initiative, tackling work that has piled up.

Jupiter (transiting): Period of expansion, exceptional opportunity for achieving success in business, receiving benefits, good favour. Afflicted: serious misjudgments likely; exaggerated, extravagant behaviour, sheer bad luck.

Saturn (transiting): Period of limitation, restriction, possible ill-health, depleted energy, losses, depressive moods, death, general misfortune. Yet can also be a useful time for wise long-term planning, conserving energy, building up resources, study, serious contemplation of life and self. Patience, tolerance, will be needed, as this will not be a time when one can expect to push ahead with plans and affairs, and it will not be much good trying to force matters. Far better to consolidate, count one's blessings, and prepare for when more go-ahead indications are shown in one's chart.

Uranus (transiting): Period when unplanned, sudden, drastic upheavals and changes can be expected. Dramatic turn to circumstances. New way of life opens. Possible period of inspiration, originality, creativeness, unconventional and rebellious behaviour.

Neptune (transiting): Peculiar, strange, confusing, chaotic happenings likely. Great creative works have been inspired during such a period. Neurotic, escapist, suicidal, mentally-disturbed tendencies shown in the natal chart are stimulated.

Pluto (transiting): Period of major transformation in the life-pattern. Often the end of a 'chapter of experience' for the start of another, due to eruptive developments that have been 'brewing up under the surface' for a long time.

Progressed Ascendant and M.C. Unless the time of birth is very accurately known one can disregard progressing these two factors. They are calculated same as for the natal chart, except that the noon sidereal time for Greenwich for *progressed year* is used, together with the time and place of birth. Both Ascendant and M.C. will be seen to have progressed forward, perhaps into another sign, which implies noticeable development of the new sign's traits (though those of birth Ascendant or M.C. will always be dominant). Aspects formed by progressed Ascendant suggest significant developments of self-centred interests, personal ambitions, health; progressed M.C., career and business interests of special importance.

Linda's Progressions and Transits Interpreted. Here are the major progressed aspects you should have found; also the most important major transits I have listed:

1962: ☉ into ♌; ♃ tr. ☌ Asc.; ♅ tr. ☍ Asc.; ☉$_P$ P ♄$_P$.
1963: ☉$_P$ P ♀; ☿$_P$ P ♀$_P$; ♃ tr. □ ☉; ♅ tr. ☍ Asc., □ ♀ ♄; ☉$_P$ P ♄.
1964: ☉$_P$ ⚹ ♅, P ☿; ☿$_P$ △ ☽; ♅ tr. □ ♀ ♄; ♄ tr. ☌ Asc.
1965: ☉$_P$ ⚹ ♅$_P$; ♄ tr. ☌ Asc., □ ♀ ♄.

Actually in 1960, the critical year in her life, the climax of her relationship with the father of her child, and the undoubted start of a 'new chapter of her life' with the birth of her child, there were the following major aspects:

♇ tr. ☌ 7th cusp, □ ♀ ♄; ☉p P ♅; ♄ tr. ☍ ☉.

The Sun-Uranus aspect indicated increasing interest in unconventional, original and dramatic forms of self-expression, that could result in drastic and unplanned incidents – and, particularly as Uranus is in conjunction Venus natally, break-up of a personal relationship. In itself this aspect need not have corresponded with a too-drastic happening, since Sun-Uranus were unaspected together at birth. But at the same time, because of this lack of natal contact, she would have been likely to have had less conscious control of the Sun-Uranus factor within herself, i.e., to direct this stimulated impulse in the way she wanted to use it. This aspect probably had greater effect, however, because at the same time Pluto by transit formed that powerful contact with 7th cusp, Venus and Saturn. Although it was naturally a bad enough experience for such a youngster to ultimately have to have her child adopted, we might say that because Pluto was natally sextile to Venus-Saturn things did not turn out so bad as they might have done. The restriction, worry, added responsibility and privation of this period is very clearly suggested by transiting Saturn opposing natal Sun.

During 1962 opportunities for distinct improvement would be likely with transiting Jupiter conjoining Ascendant; and Sun progressing into Leo points to the gradual development of a more masterful and self-assured handling of her life. Progressed Sun and Saturn forming a mutual parallel aspect indicates the need during 1962–63 for self-restraint, control and sensible planning of her life, as well as acceptance of any limitations, rather than to let these upset her and try to fight against them. It could coincide with undermining of health, if she does not take the warning of this aspect. Here is just one example of how one can apply astrology positively and helpfully! The transit of Uranus into the 7th house (marriage, intimate associations) automatically causes an opposition aspect to the Ascendant. Since Uranus-Asc. were in square aspect natally great care will be needed with regard to personal relationships, if another drastic upset is to be avoided during 1962–63.

Very certainly 1963 will be an important and even further critical year for our Linda. Progressed Sun will be parallel to Venus, and progressed Mercury will be parallel to progressed Venus: her powerful feeling-nature will be likely to dominate and influence her actions and general behaviour. A very close new tie of affection could be formed, but . . . in late-1963 and during 1964 transiting Uranus will be square to Venus-Saturn, with which Uranus is conjoined natally. This is going to be a great test of her ability to positively control this potent Uranus-Venus-Saturn feature in her make-up. Sun-Jupiter were powerfully conjoined at birth, and the square of Jupiter to Sun during 1963 may well attract her into circumstances where wise judgment will be absolutely necessary if she is to avoid loss of prestige or even a temporary lowering of her standard of living.

From the point of view of her interest in art there should be good prospects for her to obtain an opening in this field in 1963.

And so we can go on predicting the trends in her life, for as many years ahead that we want to. The pattern is already pre-determined, yet it is not a case of fate that cannot be avoided, but with this knowledge of future patterns one can plan, know in which direction problems are most likely to arise, and so offset what might be personal disaster or tragedy.

New Moons. I have not considered these with regard to the 1963 trends for Linda, but these aspects are always worth noting. Always on the left-hand pages of *Raphael's Ephemerides* you will find the date and time of the New Moon for the month concerned. You do not need to calculate this Sun-Moon conjunction exactly, unless you want to, but simply note the position of the Sun for the day of the New Moon. Relate this position to the natal chart, and see if it forms an aspect with any planet allowing an orb of no more than 2°. Interpret the aspect as usual, based on the principles of the bodies involved. This can be a good time for starting an important new venture, especially if the New Moon conjoins the natal Ascendant, M.C. or Sun.

15

Some further definitions

Detriment. A planet is said to be weak when in the opposite sign to the sign it rules: it is in a sign detrimental to its ease of expression. Whether this traditional belief has any value depends upon how you *think* about the planets and signs. The way I interpret the planets and signs as functions within the human Psyche it is grossly misleading to immediately consider a planet weak when in its 'sign of detriment'. Saturn is in its detriment in Cancer. How absurd to say Saturn, the function it represents in man, is going to be weak. It could prove to be a function of tremendous importance in the development of a powerful character, because it will bring *control* to what is essentially an emotional attitude (Cancer).

Electional, Inceptional charts. If it is desired to calculate a chart for a given moment when some action is to be taken, a business started, a ship launched, *when the question of choice of time does not arise because already decided on*, this is called an *inceptional* chart.

When an astrologer is asked to *choose* a favourable time for some action, perhaps a wedding, the formation of a business, an important journey, within a certain limited period, this is called an *electional* chart.

Exalted. A planet is said to be strong when in a sign in which it is 'exalted', because the nature of the sign has a certain affinity with the principle of the planet. Again this is a traditional idea that can lead to misjudgment, and in my opinion should be ignored. A planet can function purposively in each of the signs; whether it does depends upon aspects received, the whole chart pattern, and the positive reactions of the individual concerned. Traditionally:

$\odot$ is exalted in ♈
☽ is exalted in ♉
☿ is exalted in ♍

♀ is exalted in ♓
♂ is exalted in ♑
♃ is exalted in ♋
♄ is exalted in ♎

Fall. The sign of a planet's fall is that opposite to the sign of its exaltation, therefore, traditionally the planet is said to be weak. This idea should be ignored. To say that all Sun-Librans apply the Sun-factor weakly, and not as a positive integrating faculty, balanced with other factors, is absurd.

Horary astrology. You have a problem, or you receive a letter containing a direct question, so you calculate a chart for this very moment, which is supposed to supply the answer to your problem or question. In my opinion this is not astrology. Each moment in time may possess a distinct quality and be the link between past and present, but this is sheer nonsense for anyone to believe that a question written down at, say, 4.31 p.m. on Tuesday, has its correct answer wrapped neatly in cosmic vibrations turned in to when the letter is opened on Wednesday, 9.30 a.m. – or, if the recipient's train was held up on the way to his office, at 9.14 a.m. Horary astrology makes a mockery of a serious subject.

Mundane astrology. A specialised branch of astrology dealing with political and mundane affairs of any country and the world in general. Usually the charts used for predicting the future affairs of a country are: the chart cast for the time the State was formed (if known), the charts of its ruler and heads of government. An extremely useful branch of astrology worthy of research and practical investigation.

Mutual Reception. When each of two planets is placed in the sign ruled by the other. It is said this relationship is as if they were in conjunction. This is too strong an assertion, and appears to be an unnecessary complication rather than a correlative and recognisable feature in the character of the individual. Example: Mars in Virgo, Mercury in Aries.

Obliquity of Ecliptic. The angle between the plane of the ecliptic and the plane of the equator. At the present time this angle or value is about 23° 27′ and it is diminishing at the rate of about 47″ per century. It is equal to half the difference of the meridian altitude of the Sun at mid-summer and mid-winter. Its principal effect is the production of the seasons.

Precession of the Equinoxes. Is caused by the gravitational attraction of the Sun and Moon on the protuberant matter at the Earth's equator. Thus there is a slow retrograde motion of the Equinoctial Points along the ecliptic caused by the tilting of the Earth's axis, though the yearly increase is a mere 50". The complete retrograde cycle of the Equinoctial Points around the ecliptic takes about 25 800 years. It is because of Precession that astrology is frequently debunked by those sceptics who think the zodiacal signs are the constellations of the same names, who point out that when an astrologer says the Sun is in Aries 0° (at Spring Equinox) it is actually in the constellation Pisces 5° at the present time.

Rectification. An attempt to determine a speculative time of birth when this is not known. There are various systems, though I have found the most reliable to be the relating of the major transiting planets and the progressed Moon to past events of importance in the life of the individual. I ask the client for a dozen or more dates and details of events in their life such as marriage, deaths of close associates, love affairs, illness or accident, major changes, and referring to the *Ephemerides* relative to these dates find if any of the planets (Jupiter to Pluto) by transit might have formed an aspect (corresponding to the nature of the event) to a degree which could be either the Ascendant or M.C. Similarly with the progressed Moon. Transit of planets through certain houses at the time of events should be considered. A serious illness can often be traced to the Ascendant, and physical characteristics associated with this speculative sign checked with a photo of the person.

Sidereal Zodiac. A zodiac of the constellations, Aries 0° corresponding to the beginning of the constellation Aries, followed by arbitrary divisions of 30°, regardless of the true size and overlapping of these groups of stars. This zodiac as applied at the present time in this country by a few sincere astrologers has invariably completely fallen down whenever I have tested it with the data of persons I know. The idea seems quite illogical. Why start with the constellation Aries, anyway? With the *Tropical Zodiac* (the one used in this book) the signs begin at a distinct and logical point: the intersection of ecliptic and equator at the Spring Equinox. I cannot vouch for the value of the systems used with the Sidereal Zodiac in eastern countries, having not studied these.

Southing. Astronomically the Sun is said to *south* at noon. Any celestial body the moment it crosses the upper meridian of a place is *southing* that meridian. Beginners in astrology are usually puzzled as to why South is indicated as the top of the astrological chart and North the bottom. The observer is supposed to stand facing South, thus East is on the *left* (Ascendant) where the Sun rises above the horizon, whence it moves in correct sequence to the South, then dips below the horizon in the West, on the *right* of the chart.

Synastry. (Gk.: *syn*, together with, *astron*, a star.) The comparison of one person's chart with that of someone else, or between the charts of several individuals. This is an extremely valuable feature of astrology. Frequently I am asked to compare the charts of a couple engaged to be married; or of two men considering going into business partnership. The planets of one chart are each in turn related by sign and degree with the planets in the other chart, and any aspects noted exactly as if the planets were in the one chart. In this way a very true picture emerges of the degree of compatibility or incompatibility, and the most likely source of conflict or sympathy within the natures. Besides aspects (which, incidentally, are only allowed a maximum orb of 3° with synastry) the Ascending, Sun and Moon signs may be compared, whilst the houses of one chart in which the planets of the other chart fall can indicate directions of mutual interests. Especially in the case of emotional friendships, one can usually see whether the relationship is likely to last, or that it is just a passing infatuation, by checking individual progressions and transits and also relating the progressed positions of A's planets with the natal planets in B's chart, and vice versa, during the period when interest was aroused in one another. Tactful advice and guidance can then be given.

16

Two case-histories

Miss Marilyn Monroe. Some time between 8–9 p.m., 4th August 1962, Marilyn Monroe, the beautiful, talented film-actress, died from an overdose of barbiturates. An autopsy showed that her body contained nearly twice as much barbiturate as was necessary to kill her.

Neptune is invariably prominent in the charts of those whose death is surrounded in mystery, and was a dominant psychological feature throughout the tragic life-span of 36 years of Hollywood's 'sex symbol', as she was called. Officially she died of an overdose, yet the mystery remains. When her body was found she was clutching a white telephone, still on its hook. Perhaps, desperate for sleep (she suffered severely from insomnia) she had taken the heavy dose of barbiturates, and then realised it could be a fatal dose – had clutched for the telephone to ring for help, but too late. We shall never know.

Psychologically she had suicidal-tendencies (the powerful Ψ on her Ascendant, ☍ ☽ ♃, □ ♄; and (☽ ☌ ♃) □ ♄ indicating the severe depressive moods she would experience). Shortly after her death the *New York Post* reported that Miss Monroe had made four attempts on her own life. Three times by overdoses of sleeping pills, once by turning on a gas fire in her apartment. She once confided to a friend that she had attempted suicide twice before she was 19. There is an above-average risk of accidents or death through gas, drugs, with those persons whose birth-chart has a dominant Ψ feature. And, according to whether other factors in their make-up (strong factors in the chart) enable them to control and direct this Ψ function into positive, practical expression, so are these persons likely to seek drastic relief and escape from problems and emotional and mental distress.

Ψ indicates the sensitivity and impressionableness of her nature; its contact with ♌ Asc. ♀ ♃ ☽ her potential talents as an artist. ☉ ☌ ☿ shows versatility and a restless, active mind. Psychologically, other

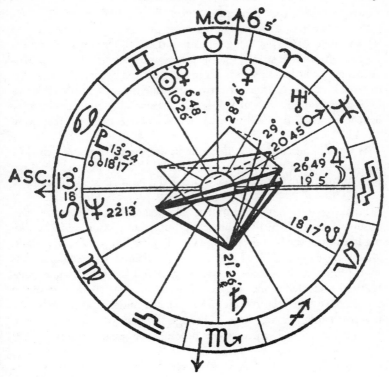

FIGURE 11

Birth-chart: Marilyn Monroe
Born 9.30 a.m. P.S.T.,
1st June 1926,
Los Angeles

than the ♉ M.C., her make-up lacked the down-to-earth, stabilising control of the Earth element, so necessary for 'harnessing' the powerful ♆ function. Under stress the ☉ ☿/♊ feature would quickly tend to create nervous excitability, diffused thinking. It is not improbable that the otherwise unaspected ☉ ☌ ☿ predisposed to a form of dissociation of the thought-processes under extreme emotional and mental distress, undermined by the 'disintegrative' processes of ♆.

Progressed and transiting indications for August 1962 present a critical pattern. Throughout most of July 1962 transiting ♆ was 'stationary' at *exact* parallel aspect with natal ♃; progressed ☽ ⊼ ♄.

Exactly formed major progressed aspects during 1962 were: ☉$_{P}$ ☌ ♇$_{P}$ (a drastic bringing to an end of a chapter of experience) in 12th house (of self-undoing); ♀$_{P}$ ☌ ☉$_{r}$ (stimulating the emotional nature and reactions when under stress); ☿$_{P}$ P ☽$_{r}$ (nervous-emotional stimulus). Miss Monroe's birth-data I received from an American source, the time said to have been taken from her birth certificate. Possibly this could be a few minutes either side of 9.30 a.m., thereby suggesting that ☿ may have progressed by 1962 to exact conjunction Ascendant, if it were ♌ 11°.

♄ in 4th house, □ ☽ ♃ in 7th, indicates the misery, and denial of parental love, she experienced as a child in 11 foster homes; her three broken marriages; and the loss of her child (also afflicted ♃, ruler of 5th).

Frankie Vaughan had said of her: 'She was the complete star, but so unsure of herself.' (♆.) Unpunctuality, ultimately resulting in her being fired from the film *Something's Got To Give* just prior to her death, we can trace to (♆ ☌ Asc.) ☍ ☽. She was a talented, tormented, restless soul, professionally successful, yet ever denied the security and sanctuary of love, that it was tragically ironical her last, uncompleted film should have that title. Astrologically we can understand the crisis she had reached in her life, viewed through the sensitivity and tension of her natal chart, and when tension becomes too great *something's got to give*.

A Nursing career. Fig. 12 is the chart of a relative of the author. Her whole life was spent nursing in hospitals (Asc. ☉ ☿ ♂ in ♍; ☉ ♅ ♀ in 12th), or as matron of orphanages (strong ♃ in 5th). For a period she was assistant-matron of a well-known London hospital; for several years matron of a girls' orphanage both in England and Canada (M.C. and ♇ in 9th): important new phase of experience connected with abroad).

She did not marry until her mid-forties (♄ (☍ ☿, Asc./☉ ruler) in 7th). For 2 years she was wonderfully happy with her husband, then suddenly he died. ♄ in 7th denied her a lasting marriage, but ♄ ✱ ♃ suggests the deep happiness of the brief experience even so. ☽ ☍ ♆, □ ♃ (♆ ♃ co-rulers of 7th) also indicate the likelihood of the marriage-pattern being broken. She never had children of her own.

Around middle-age she was operated on for carcinoma of the ovaries (☽ ♏). She died 23rd April 1960 of inoperable carcinoma of the liver (☽ □ ♃). Her spiritualist faith gave her great strength as she lay dying. As a trained nurse she knew exactly what was happening

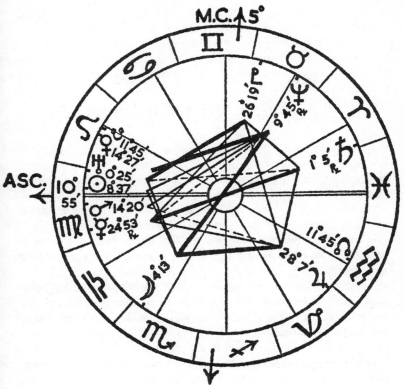

FIGURE 12

Birth-chart: Female
Born 5.30 a.m.
1st September 1878
Nr. Barnstaple, England

throughout her final illness. A week before she died, knowing she
would soon not be able to think clearly because of the pain-killing
drugs, she gave full instructions for the removal of her body from the
house as soon as she died ('You don't want my old cast-off shell hanging
around') and the disposal of her ashes, and wrote her own obituary, to
be sent to a London daily newspaper!

She was a powerful, dominating woman ((☉ ☌ ♂) ☌ Asc.), inclined
to be very critical, expecting absolute efficiency of herself and others
(strong ♍).

17

Astrology today and tomorrow

If astrology is all it is claimed to be, you may have thought whilst reading this book, why is it not an accepted science, taught in universities, applied by every psychologist as the very basis for his understanding of a client's personal problem or neurosis?

Ignorance of the true facts of astrology is the main reason, which state of affairs is not helped by the 'lucky star' features in the daily newspapers.

There are, today, two courses open for the truths of astrology to become more widely realised, and the subject ultimately - as it must inevitably be - established as an essential subject to be taught in all schools and universities.

(a) For those *soundly trained* in the subject to spread its truths by means of analyses prepared for other people, who (and I can speak from experience of my own clients) will be so impressed they will either desire to study astrology themselves or recommend friends to have a similar analysis prepared from their individual birth-data;

(b) For intensive scientific statistical research to be undertaken by competent astrologers in co-operation with the authorities of whatever field of human affairs is being correlated to astrological factors.

I was one of twenty astrologers from the United Kingdom and the United States participating in an experiment devised by Mr. Vernon Clark, an American psychologist.[1] The entire project was proctored by two Ph.D.'s and diplomates in clinical psychology.

We astrologers were asked to match ten birth-charts with ten case-histories describing occupations. A control group (persons knowing nothing about astrology) were given the same charts and case-histories, their matchings of course being sheer chance.

[1] See details in *Astrology and Commonsense*, by Ingrid Lind (Hodder & Stoughton, 1962).

The experiment was highly successful for the astrologers, 16 out of the 20 predicting better than chance, against 9 out of the control group 20.

John H. Nelson, radio meteorologist for RCA Communications, Inc., predicts with 93 per cent. of accuracy electromagnetic storms, which are correlated to traditional angular relationships of the planets and the Sun.

The correlation of sun-spot cycles, with particular consideration to the phases of maximum and minimum sun-spot activity, with rainfall and certain epidemics have attracted the interest of scientists and meteorologists for more than a century, with intriguing results. A study of the fluctuations in the growth of trees as recorded by their annual growth-rings has shown a correspondence with the fluctuations of rainfall cycles, corresponding to the 11-year rhythm' of sun-spots.

With scientific evidence that the cyclic motions and inter-relationships of the Sun, Moon and planets correspond to growth-patterns in vegetative forms of Earth-life, and with meteorological phenomena, one cannot discount the possibility of the human being, physically and psychologically, also being a part of these inter-related patterns of Earth and cosmic energy-systems.

It is for the astrologers to present the evidence justifying their theories on the rigid terms demanded by science. Unfortunately many scientists are reluctant to accept astrological evidence even when proof is given them. A typical example occurred in 1962. In *Science* (Vol. 137) two groups of scientists – in Australia and America – reported their research into the influence of the Moon's phases upon rainfall. Neither group knew the other was making a similar study, yet both achieved the same results. They discovered that heavy rain occurs most frequently in the weeks immediately following New Moon and Full Moon, based on thousands of records from 1500 weather stations over the period 1900–49. The results so surprised the Australian group that *they refrained from publishing observations for fear of ridicule from other scientists*! In short, their investigation was astrological: the interpretation of the Moon's effects upon natural Earth phenomena.

In the scientific journal *Nature* (Supplement No. 4, Vol. 184) Dr. Rudolph Tomaschek, a retired University of Munich geophysicist, reported his findings of a study of the 134 most powerful earthquakes (above magnitude $7\frac{3}{4}$) during the period 1904–6. He found that the planet Uranus (astrologically associated with disruptive, unexpected, explosive occurrences) was within 15° of the upper or lower meridian of an earthquake's epicentre far more frequently than chance would allow.

There is not a field of human experience in which astrological interpretation cannot be developed along strictly scientific lines of investigation.

There can be little doubt that astrology will, tomorrow, be an accepted feature of life, just as today once-ridiculed psychology is accepted as a valuable contribution to man's understanding of his own mental and emotional processes of behaviour.

It will be for the scientist to unravel the mystery of synchronicity; for the ordinary man and woman, parents, psychologists, probation officers, schoolteachers, the vital key to understanding the growing child or the delinquent youth will be that of the individual birthmoment, necessitating a one-year's course in basic astrological principles and theory.

Dr. Carl Jung, in a letter in 1948 to the Editor of the Indian *Astrological Magazine*, confessed his faith in astrology: '. . . I've been interested in this particular activity of the human mind since more than 30 years. As I am a psychologist, I'm chiefly interested in the particular light the horoscope sheds on certain complications in the character. In cases of difficult psychological diagnosis I usually get a horoscope in order to have a further point of view from an entirely different angle. I must say that I very often found that the astrological data elucidated certain points which I otherwise would have been unable to understand.'

When this chapter was first written in 1962, 1979 was indeed part of 'tomorrow'. During these intervening years much extremely favourable and convincing astrological research has been accomplished.

Three areas of research must be mentioned. Michel Gauquelin, a French psychologist and statistician, with his wife and a band of helpers, undertook a monumental statistical analysis of the birth-data of many thousands of famous persons. In the field of vocation they confirmed traditional astrological theories regarding the angular placing of Mars (with sports champions), Saturn (with famous doctors and scientists), and Jupiter (with famous actors). Their analysis of the birth-data of 30 000 French parents and their children showed that a 'planetary heredity effect' exists.

The British astrologer, John Addey, has pioneered research into the application of harmonic analysis in astrology, with exciting prospects. To quote Addey, harmonic analysis is the study of 'The rhythms and sub-rhythms of cosmic periods, which can be demonstrated to provide the basis for all astrological doctrine both ancient and modern'.

And in chapter 18, you can read of the highly successful research undertaken by myself with the cooperation of Professor Hans Eysenck.

18

Eysenck-Mayo research study

One of the oldest and most important astrological theories states that the six *odd*-numbered zodiacal signs (Aries, Gemini, Leo, Libra, Sagittarius, Aquarius) tend towards *extraversion*, while the six *even*-numbered signs (Taurus, Cancer, Virgo, Scorpio, Capricorn, Pisces) tend towards *introversion*. For example, persons born with the Sun in Gemini would be far more likely to develop an extraverted type of personality than would persons born with the Sun in Taurus.

Writers from other centuries – and, indeed, most astrological writers up to recent times – did not use the terms 'extraversion' or 'introversion', but their description of traits associated with the signs left no doubts as to these two basic attitudes being described.

The typical extravert:

is sociable;
likes parties; has many friends;
needs to have people to talk to;
does not like reading or studying by himself;
craves excitement; takes chances;
is generally impulsive;
always has a ready answer;
is carefree, easy-going, optimistic;
prefers to be active and doing things.

The typical introvert:

is quiet and retiring, introspective;
fond of books rather than people;
is reserved and distant except to intimate friends;
tends to plan ahead;
does not like taking chances;

does not like excitement or bustle;
takes matters of everyday life seriously;
keeps his feelings under close control;
likes a well-ordered mode of life.

The pilot study

In 1969 I set out to prove conclusively that these two basic attitudes of extraversion-introversion can be associated with alternate zodiacal signs. As a practising astrologer I knew from my personal experience of thousands of birth-charts of known individuals that this was a valid theory, but sound statistical evidence was needed to help convince critics of astrology. The very best test would be to have individuals indicate personally that they possessed particular traits associated with either extraversion or introversion, though without knowing that these two personality dimensions were being tested astrologically. I compiled a questionnaire of 74 questions, half of these relating to traits associated with extraversion, and half relating to introversion. These questions were based on traits listed in the writings of a large number of the world's leading psychologists, and the traits were those which most or all of the psychologists were agreed upon.

The Mayo School of Astrology, with students in over one hundred countries, has an enormous daily postbag from students and from those enquiring for details of the correspondence courses. This was to be an ideal source from which to gather completed questionnaires. Correspondents and their friends or relatives were invited to co-operate in the research study by completing a questionnaire and supplying their birth-data (date, place, and if possible, time of birth). The way that a person answered the question would then be related to the various factors in their birth-chart, particularly to those factors drawn on by astrologers for the interpretation of a person's tendency to either extraversion or introversion.

Over a period of about one year several thousand questionnaires were enclosed with the normal outgoing letters from the School. A total of 1795 completed questionnaires were returned and used in the pilot study. These came from persons from all walks of life, from over thirty different countries (both northern and southern hemispheres), and were indeed a fair and random cross-section of society. It was evident that women responded far more readily than men to participate in this study, in the ratio of 2:1.

The initial test was to examine the Sun's positions in each of the twelve signs in regard to the tendency to either extraversion or intro-version. Naturally one would never expect *all* persons with the Sun in odd-numbered signs to be distinctly extraverted, nor *all* persons with the Sun in even-numbered signs to be definitely introverted. As you will find from your study of this book, many more astrological factors are needed than simply the Sun-sign to determine the detailed psychological potentialities of an individual. This would also apply to extraverted and introverted traits. The analysis of all factors is at present under review. It is a complex task, but one that should prove immensely valuable and reveal the reason why, for instance, a particular individual with the Sun in an odd-numbered sign is excessively extraverted, and why another individual with the Sun also in an odd-numbered sign is just the opposite – excessively introverted.

The results were tremendously successful, and the graph depicting the 'saw-tooth' pattern of the signs as being alternately extraverted and introverted when 'occupied' by the Sun was, for me, beautiful!

This graph is illustrated in Figure 13 by the *broken* lines. The horizontal line represents the mean or average of the total scores from the 1795 samples, males and females combined. The signs above this mean line show a tendency to extraversion, the signs below this line show a tendency to introversion. As you can see, the six odd-numbered signs are all above the mean line, whilst the six even-numbered signs are all below this line. Sagittarius is shown to be more frequently extraverted of all the signs, followed closely by Aries; whereas the least extraverted signs are Virgo and Pisces.

I wanted the data to be independently tested statistically, preferably by an authority of distinction in the field of psychology. I chose Professor Hans Eysenck, Director of the Department of Psychology in the Institute of Psychiatry in London.

When his Institute's computer analysed the data he was profoundly surprised by the results. The odds against the results being arrived at by chance were over 10 000 to 1. Such a very high level of significance was clearly a challenge to a distinguished psychologist to test astrology further, and a breakthrough of considerable importance had already been achieved in the long journey to ultimately get astrology taught in universities and schools.

The second study

It was understandable that Professor Eysenck wanted to repeat the study before committing himself to an acknowledgment of the validity

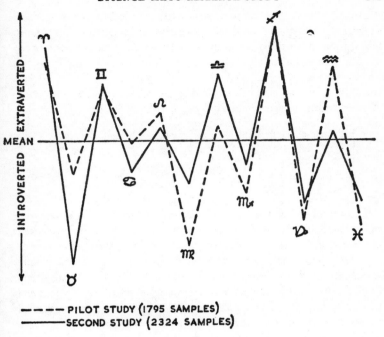

FIGURE 13

Sun-sign correlation with Extraversion-Introversion tendencies

of the astrological theory concerning extraversion–introversion. In the second study we used his universally recognised E.P.I. (Eysenck Personality Inventory). This inventory or questionnaire endeavours to measure two major dimensions of personality: extraversion-introversion, and neuroticism (emotionality or stability-instability). Thus, as well as repeating the test of the hypothesis that the position of the Sun in each of the twelve zodiacal signs at the time of birth shows a tendency, alternately, to a predisposition to extraversion and introversion, we were also testing another centuries-old astrological theory concerning the three *Water* signs (Cancer, Scorpio, Pisces).

This theory states that persons born with either of the three Water signs prominent in their birth-chart will tend more to emotionalism or neuroticism than persons born with any of the other signs prominent.

What exactly does this questionnaire measure in terms of neuroticism? A person who 'scores high' on the emotionality or neuroticism scale is not, of course, necessarily a neurotic; but there is a certain predisposition to neurosis, which does not imply an actual neurotic breakdown. One might think of neuroticism as suggesting a person who is *anxiety-prone*.

Neuroticism is characterised by:

> mood swings; lack of concentration;
> worries and anxieties;
> psychosomatic symptoms;
> nervousness; sensitivity;
> inferiority feelings.

The main source of samples for the second study was again through the Mayo School of Astrology. Much of the outgoing correspondence contained questionnaires, and after about a year I had collected 2324 samples together with the necessary birth-data. It should be pointed out that in both studies only about a third of the questionnaires were from persons who had an understanding of astrology. Statistically there was found to be no difference (or bias) between their scores and the scores of those who had no understanding of astrology.

When the data from the second study of 2324 samples were analysed at the Institute of Psychiatry, the same significant results correlating extraversion-introversion with alternate signs were obtained as in the pilot study. This can be clearly seen in the *unbroken* line in Figure 13. The sign-type tending most to extraversion is again shown to be Sagittarius, while the Taurean subjects indicated in their answers that they tend to be more introverted than any other sign-type. Again, only the six odd-numbered signs score *above* the average or mean score for the total of 2324 samples, whilst the six even-numbered signs each score *less* than the average. Once more the traditional astrological theory was shown to be valid, after sound statistical testing, and again the odds against the results being arrived at by chance were over 10 000 to 1.

Highly significant results were also achieved in the prediction of the three Water signs tending to be more neurotically-inclined than the other signs. When portrayed in graph form in Figure 14 only these three Water signs and Aries are above the mean-score line. The fact that the Sun-Aries types also scored very high on the neuroticism scale would be no surprise to the astrologer. We know how highly emo-

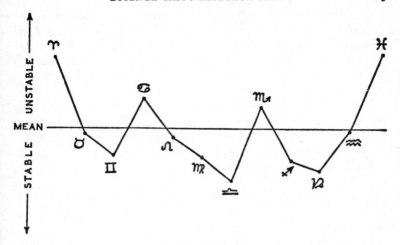

FIGURE 14

Sun-sign correlation with a tendency to Neuroticism

tional and unstable the Aries type can be, although this is a Fire sign and not a Water sign.

Just how immensely significant these results are, and how beautifully, in graph form, these traditional astrological theories are confirmed, may be realised if we bear in mind that each of the 2324 individuals participating in the second study indicated 'yes' or 'no' against 24 questions relating to extraverted traits. 2324 persons between the ages of sixteen and about seventy, from all walks of life and from over thirty different countries, answered a grand total of 55 776 questions. Critics of astrology might well have predicted any of several thousand chaotic and chance results. But just as our astrological ancestors would have predicted many centuries ago, the results produced the graph illustrated in Figure 13. The same can be said about the Water signs and emotional inclinations.

With the wonders of the Space-Age, television pictures from the Moon's surface, rockets to the most distant planets, creating for the human mind a fresh dimension in thought-experience and imagination, man's physical exploration into distant areas of the solar system knows no bounds. And now, after centuries of being dismissed as nonsense by the uninformed, astrology, too, has brought man to the threshold of another new dimension of experience: the realisation of our physiological, biological and psychological relationship with our cosmic environment. The doors are being flung open for sincere, open-minded co-operation between competent astrologers, psychologists, scientists, and the medical profession to research the claims of astrology and together to construct a new science.

As Professor Eysenck said about our second research study in an article in the London *Evening Standard* of 2nd March 1977, which was distributed world-wide by the Associated Press: '. . . when the results were put through the computer the predicted relations between personality and birth date did in fact come out very clearly.

'I must admit that this was a great surprise to me . . . my instinctive scepticism and dislike of anything mystical had led me to expect unrelieved failure from any investigations of astrological predictions. To find some solid fact in the astrological field was surprising and not entirely welcome . . . .

'In due course no doubt someone will be able to think up a plausible reason for these uncomfortable findings; so far all we have are these mysterious but to me at least fascinating glimpses of aspects of reality which scientists so far have refused to look at. Perhaps our arrogance has been misplaced: there may indeed be more things in heaven and earth than we have dreamt of!'

The result of my research with Professor Eysenck were given in a jointly written paper published in 1978 in Volume 105 of the *American Journal of Social Psychology*. The paper is entitled: *An Empirical Study of the Relation between Astrological Factors and Personality*, by J. Mayo, O. White and H. J. Eysenck (University of London).

Appendices

APPENDIX I

Recommended Reading

The Modern Textbook of Astrology, by Margaret Hone (L. N. Fowler & Co. Ltd.). The main textbook of the Mayo School of Astrology.

Applied Astrology, by Margaret Hone (L. N. Fowler & Co. Ltd.). Companion book to the above.

Books by Jeff Mayo (L. N. Fowler & Co. Ltd.):

The Astrologer's Astronomical Handbook . . . Vividly describing the astronomical framework upon which astrological theories are based.

How to Read the Ephemeris . . . Clearly explains how to understand and apply the mass of data in Raphael's ephemerides.

How to Cast a Natal Chart . . . Everything one wants to know about constructing a birth-chart, with helpful exercises (and answers).

The Planets and Human Behaviour . . . A fresh, penetrating insight to the Sun, Moon and planets and what these represent in the chart and in basic psychological terms.

These books are of particular value to beginners, each volume giving detailed explanations in an easy-to-follow style.

Harmonics in Astrology, by John Addey (L. N. Fowler & Co. Ltd.).
Recent Advances in Natal Astrology, by Geoffrey Dean.

Essential Reference Books

Raphael's Ephemerides (W. Foulsham & Co. Ltd.). Any one year from 1860 to date.

Raphael's Tables of Houses for Gt. Britain (Lats. 50° 22′N to 59°N). (W. Foulsham & Co. Ltd.).

Raphael's Tables of Houses for Northern Latitudes (Lats. 0°–50°N). (W. Foulsham & Co. Ltd.).

Pluto Ephemeris (1840–1960), by Benjamine (The Aries Press).

Pluto Tables (1851–2000), by Ebertin (Ebertin–Verlag, Aalen).

Philips' New Practical Atlas, containing a gazetteer giving co-ordinates for 35 000 towns and cities.

Knowledge of the correct Standard Time or Daylight Saving Time (or Summer Time) operative at a given date is vitally important for the astrologer, and these three volumes by Doris Doane are an invaluable aid:

Time Changes in the World.
Time Changes in the United States.
Time Changes in Canada & Mexico.

All books listed, also printed chart-forms, can be purchased direct from:

The Mayo School of Astrology,
c/o Teach Yourself Books

For a Book List, write enclosing a stamped and addressed envelope or International Reply Coupon.

APPENDIX II

The Mayo School of Astrology

In the field of astrological teaching Jeff Mayo has a wealth of experience and is regarded as a leading authority. His school provides sound practical methods of study under the direct guidance of a tutor.

As a reader of this book who may be seeking a wider and more detailed study of astrology, you are invited to send for the School's Prospectus.

Tuition is solely by correspondence. On enrolment you will be placed under a tutor who will keep in close touch with you, receiving your test papers and correcting these fully, explaining mistakes.

Jeff Mayo, the Principal-Emeritus, has since 1957 personally taught students from about 150 countries – including the British Isles, the U.S.A., Australia, South Africa, Iceland, Japan, Sweden, Brazil, Canada, New Zealand, Ghana, Hawaii, Zambia, Denmark, Yugoslovia – indeed, from every corner of the globe.

The *Basic Course.* This is the course not only for beginner-students but for anyone wishing to gain a sound mastery of the basic theory and principles of astrology. On enrolment you will receive a textbook and a folder containing your complete study materials, exercises, chart forms and an ephemeris. You will be taught the astronomical framework upon which all chart calculations and astrological theories are based. You will learn how to calculate charts for births anywhere on Earth, and to interpret these in terms of potential psychological traits and future trends in the life.

On completion of the Basic Course a *Certificate of Proficiency* will be awarded to any student who has maintained a consistently high standard of work.

The *Advanced Preparatory Course*. Designed for prospective advanced students of astrology who already have a sound working knowledge of basic techniques, and who would therefore prefer to avoid having to enrol for the entire Basic Course. This has been prepared to give the student a considerable saving on normal course fees.

The *Advanced Course*. This is designed for more advanced study, as well as preparing the student for future consultative work and counselling. On completion of this course the examination for the Diploma may be taken. Successful candidates will have the right to put *D.M.S.Astrol.* (Diploma of the Mayo School of Astrology) after their names.

Book Service. Students will receive a list of recommended astrology books they may purchase.

There is a pen friends' club for Mayo School students called *Aspect Lines*. *Links* is a network of regional groups of the School's Diploma and Certificate holders, aiming to promote the study of serious astrology and astrological research, to provide a nationwide list of speakers for press, radio and TV. All Mayo School Diploma-holders are eligible to be listed in the *Astrological Consultants' Register* which is updated annually, and is available to anyone wishing to consult a qualified astrologer.

For a Prospectus, write enclosing a stamped addressed 9″ × 4″ envelope or International Reply Coupon (if you live outside Great Britain) to:

The Registrar,
The Mayo School of Astrology,
c/o Teach Yourself Books,
PO Box 702,
Dunton Green,
Sevenoaks,
Kent TN13 2YD

APPENDIX III

British Summer Times

(Changing at 2 a.m., G.M.T.)

1916	21 May	to	1 Oct.	*1947	16 March	to	2 Nov.
1917	8 April	to	17 Sept.	1948	14 „	to	31 Oct.
1918	24 March	to	30 „	1949	3 April	to	30 „
1919	30 „	to	29 „	1950	16 „	to	22 „
1920	28 „	to	25 Oct.	1951	15 „	to	21 „
1921	3 April	to	3 „	1952	20 „	to	26 „
1922	26 March	to	8 „	1953	19 „	to	4 „
1923	22 April	to	16 Sept.	1954	11 „	to	3 „
1924	13 „	to	21 „	1955	17 „	to	2 „
1925	19 „	to	4 Oct.	1956	22 „	to	7 „
1926	18 „	to	3 „	1957	14 „	to	6 „
1927	10 „	to	2 „	1958	20 „	to	5 „
1928	22 „	to	7 „	1959	19 „	to	4 „
1929	21 „	to	6 „	1960	10 „	to	2 „
1930	13 „	to	5 „	1961	26 March	tg	29 „
1931	19 „	to	4 „	1962	25 „	to	28 „
1932	17 „	to	2 „	1963	31 „	to	27 „
1933	9 „	to	8 „	1964	22 „	to	25 „
1934	22 „	to	7 „	1965	21 „	to	24 „
1935	14 „	to	6 „	1966	20 „	to	23 „
1936	19 „	to	4 „	1967	19 „	to	29 „
1937	18 „	to	3 „	1968	From 18 Feb.		
1938	10 „	to	2 „		to 31 Oct. 1971		
1939	16 „	to	19 Nov.	1972	19 March	to	29 Oct.
1940	25 Feb.	to	31 Dec.	1973	18 „	to	28 „
*1941	1 Jan.	to	31 „	1974	17 „	to	27 „
*1942	1 „	to	31 „				
*1943	1 „	to	31 „				
*1944	1 „	to	31 „				
*1945	1 „	to	7 Oct.				
1946	14 April	to	6 „				

Thereafter, from 2 a.m. G.M.T. on the third Sunday in March until 2 a.m. G.M.T. on the fourth Sunday in October.

*Double Summer Time

1941	4 May	to	10 Aug.	1945	2 April	to	15 July
1942	5 April	to	9 „	1946	No Double Summer Time		
1943	4 „	to	15 „	1947	13 April	to	10 Aug.
1944	2 „	to	17 Sept.				

APPENDIX IV

Standard Times[1]

(Corrected to October 1960)

Note. These Standard Times apply as at October 1960, but some will be different for other years. See Appendix I.

List 1: PLACES FAST ON G.M.T. (EAST OF GREENWICH)

The times given $\left\{\begin{array}{l}added\end{array}\right.$ to G.M.T. to give Standard Time.
below should be $\left\{\begin{array}{l}subtracted\end{array}\right.$ from Standard Time to give G.M.T.

	h. m.		h. m.
Aden	03	Ceylon	05 30
Admiralty Islands	10	Chagos Archipelago	05
Albania[2]	01	Chatham Islands[3]	12 45
Algeria	01	China[4]	08
Amirante Islands	04	Christmas Island, Indian	
Andaman Islands	05 30	Ocean	07
Angola (Portuguese West		Cosos–Keeling Islands	06 30
Africa)	01	Comoro Islands	03
Annoban Islands[3]	01	Congo Republic (western part,	
Australian Capital Territory	10	including Coquilhatville and	
Austria	01	Leopoldville)	01
Bahrein	04	(eastern part, including	
Ballarie Islands[3]	01	Costermansville, Elisabeth-	
Basutoland	02	ville, Lusambo and	
Bechuanaland	02	Stanleyville)	02
Belgium	01	Corsica[3]	01
British New Guinea	10	Crete	02
British North Borneo	08	Cyprus	02
British Somaliland	03	Cyrenaica[3]	02
Bulgaria	02	Czechoslovakia	01
Burma	06 30	Dahomey (French West	
Cameroons	01	Africa)	01
Caroline Islands (east of long.	10	Denmark	01
E 160°)	12	Dutch New Guinea	09 30
(west of long. E 160°)		Egypt[2]	02
(Truk, Ponape)	11		

[1] Adapted from the *Nautical Almanac* of 1963 by permission of H.M. Stationery Office.

[2] Summer time may be kept in these countries.

[3] This time is used throughout the year, but may differ from the legal time.

[4] All the coast, but some areas may keep summer time.

	h. m.		h. m.
Ellice Islands	12	Sumbawa, Talaur Is.,	
Eritrea	03	Timor	08
Estonia	03	Babar Is., Moluccas (Buru,	
Fernando Po[1]	01	Halmahera, Serang	
Fiji	12	(Ceram)), Sula Is., Wetta	08 30
Finland	02	Aru Is., Kei Is., Tanimbar	
Formosa[2]	08	Is.	09
France[1]	01	Iran (Persia)	03 30
French Equatorial Africa[3]	01	'Iraq	03
French Somaliland	03	Israel	02
Friendly Islands	12 20	Italy	01
Germany	01	Japan	09
Gibraltar[1]	01	Jappen Islands	09
Gilbert and Ellice Is.	12	Jordan	02
Greece	02	Kamchatka Peninsula	12
Guam	10	Kenya	03
Gwadar	04 30	Korea[2]	08 30
Holland	01	Kuril Islands	09
Hong Kong[2]	08	Kuweit	03
Hungary	01	Labuan	08
India	05 30	Laccadive Islands	05 30
Indo-China, Federation of		Ladrone Islands	10
Cambodia	07	Latvia	03
Laos	07	Lebanon	02
Viet Nam	08	Lichtenstein	01
Indonesia, Republic of		Lithuania	03
Mentawai Is.. Nias,		Lord Howe Island	10
Northern Sumatra	06 30	Luxembourg[1]	01
Anambas Is., Bangka,		Macao[2]	08
Belitong, Natuna Is.,		Madagascar[2]	03
Rhio Is., Southern		Malaya, Federation of	07 30
Sumatra	07	Maldive Republic	05
Bali, Borneo, Java, Lombok,		Malta	01
Madura	07 30	Manchuria	09
Alor, Celebes, Flores,		Mariana Islands	10
Lomblem, Pantar, Roti,		Marshall Islands	12
Sanghi Is., Savu, Sumba,		Mauritius	04

[1] This time is used throughout the year, but may differ from the legal time.

[2] Summer time may be kept in these countries.

[3] French Equitorial Africa includes Chad, Gabon, Middle Congo and Ubangi Shari.

	h. m.		
		Queensland	10
Monaco[1]	01	Reunion	04
Mozambique (Portuguese		Rhodesia	02
East Africa)	02		h. m.
Mukalla (Hadhramaut)	03	Rumania	02
Nanyo–Gunto	09	Russia[4] (west of long. E 40°)	03
Nauru	11 30	(long. E 40° to E 52° 30')	04
Netherlands, The	01	(east of long. E 52° 30')	05
New Caledonia	11	Sakhalin	
New Guinea, British	10	(south of lat. N 50°)	09
New Guinea, Dutch	09 30	(north of lat. N 50°)	10
New Hebrides	11	Santa Cruz Islands	11
New South Wales[2]	10	Sarawak	08
New Zealand	12	Sardinia	01
Nicobar Islands	05 30	Schouten Islands	09
Nigeria	01	Seychelles	04
Norfolk Island	11 30	Siam (Thailand)	07
North Borneo	08	Siberia[4]	
Northern Rhodesia	02	(west of long. E 67° 30')	05
Northern Territory,		(long. E 67° 30'–82° 30')	06
Australia	09 30	(long. E 82° 30'–97° 30')	07
Norway [3]	01	(long. E 97° 30'–112° 30')	08
Novaya Zemlya	05	(long. E 112° 30'–127° 30')	09
Nyasaland	02	(long. E 127° 30'–142° 30')	10
Ocean Island	11	(long. E 142° 30'–157° 30')	11
'Oman (Masira, Muscat		(long. E 157° 30'–172° 30')	12
and Salala)	04	(east of long. E 172° 30')	13
Pakistan (East)	06	Sicily	01
(West)	05	Singapore	07 30
Papua	10	Socotra	03
Pescadores Islands[3]	08	Solomon Islands	11
Philippine Republic	08	Somalia	03
Poland[3]	01	Somaliland	03
Portuguese East Africa		South Africa, Union of	02
(Mozambique)	02	South Australia	09 30
Portuguese India	05 30	Southern Rhodesia	02
Portuguese West Africa		Spain[1]	01
(Angola)	01	Spanish Guinea[1]	01
Qatar	04	Spitzbergen	01

[1] This time is used throughout the year, but may differ from the legal time.

[2] Except Broken Hill Area, which keeps 9h. 30m.

[3] Summer time may be kept in these countries.

[4] The boundaries between the zones are irregular; the longitudes given are approximate only.

	h. m.		h. m.
Sudan, Republic of	02	Trucial 'Oman (Sharja)	04
Swaziland	02	Truk	11
Sweden	01	Tunisia	01
Switzerland	01	Turkey	02
Syria[1]	02	Uganda	03
Tanganyika Territory	03	Union of South Africa	02
Tasmania	10	Victoria	10
Thailand (Siam)	07	Western Australia	08
Timor	08	Wrangell Island	13
Tonga Islands	12 20	Yugoslavia	01
Tripolitania	02	Zanzibar	03

List 2: PLACES NORMALLY KEEPING G.M.T.

Ascension Island	Mauritania
Canary Islands[2]	Morocco[1]
Channel Isles[3]	Portugal[1]
Faeroes, The	Principe
French West Africa[4]	Rio de Oro[2]
Gambia	St. Helena
Ghana	Sao Thomé
Great Britain[3]	Sierra Leone
Guinea Republic	Tangier
Ireland, Northern[3]	Togoland (Fr.)
Irish Republic[1]	Tristan da Cunha

List 3: PLACES SLOW ON G.M.T. (WEST OF GREENWICH)

The times given ⎰ *subtracted* from G.M.T. to give Standard Time.
below should be ⎱ *added* to Standard Time to give G.M.T.

	h. m.		h. m.
Alabama, U.S.A.[5]	06	Sound, Douglas, Juneau,	
Alaska, U.S.A., south-east		Kimsham Cove and Peters-	
coast to and including Cross		burg	08

[1] Summer time may be kept in these countries.

[2] G.M.T. is in general use throughout the year, but the legal standard time differs from G.M.T.

[3] Summer time is kept.

[4] Comprises: Ivory Coast, Niger, Senegal, French Sudan and Upper Volta; for Dahomey see List 1.

[5] Summer (daylight-saving) time, one hour fast on the time given, is kept in some parts of the U.S.A., especially in the east and in the metropolitan areas. The dates of beginning and end are normally the last Sunday in April and the last Sunday in September or October, at 2h. 00m. local clock time.

	h. m.		h. m.
coast northward of Cross Sound to long. W 141°	09	Cook Isles (except Nive)	10 30
		Costa Rica	06
long. W 141° to W 162° including Anchorage,		Cuba	05
		Curaçao Island	04 30
Fairbanks, Seward, Valdez	10	Delaware, U.S.A.[4]	05
Alberta[1]	07	Dominican Republic[7]	05
Aleutian Islands	11	Dutch Guiana (Surinam)	03 30
Argentina[2]	03	Ecuador	05
Arizona[3], U.S.A.[4]	07	Falkland Islands[8]	04
Arkansas, U.S.A.[4]	06	Bases in Graham Land	03
Austral Islands[5]	10	Fanning Island	10
Azores[1]	02	Fernando Noronha	02
Bahamas	05	Florida[3], U.S.A.[4]	05
Barbados	04	French Guiana	04
Bermuda	04	Georgia, U.S.A.[4]	05
Bolivia	04	Greenland, Scoresby	
Brazil (Central)	04	Sound	02
(Eastern)[6]	03	Angmagssalik and W.	
(Western)	05	Coast	03
British Columbia[1]	08	Thule area	04
British Guiana	03 45	Grenada[1]	04
British Honduras[7]	06	Guadeloupe	04
California, U.S.A.[4]	08	Guatemala	06
Canada (see provinces)		Guiana, British	03 45
Cape Verde Islands	02	„ Dutch	03 30
Cayman Islands	05	„ French	04
Chile	04	Haiti	05
Christmas Islands		Hawaiian Islands (except	
(Gilbert and Ellice)	10	Midway Islands)	10
Colombia	05	Honduras	06
Colorado, U.S.A.[4]	07	Honduras, British[7]	06
Connecticut, U.S.A.[4]	05	Iceland[1]	01

[1] Summer time may be kept in these countries.

[2] This time is used throughout the year, but may differ from the legal time.

[3] This applies to the greater portion of the state.

[4] Summer (daylight-saving) time, one hour fast on the time given, is kept in some parts of the U.S.A., especially in the east and in the metropolitan areas. The dates of beginning and end are normally the last Sunday in April and the last Sunday in September or October, at 2h. 00m. local clock time.

[5] This is the legal standard time, but local mean time is generally used.

[6] Including all the coast.

[7] Winter time may be kept in these countries.

[8] Port Stanley keeps summer time October to March.

	h. m.		h. m.
Idaho[3], U.S.A.[2]	07	Newfoundland[3]	03 30
Illinois, U.S.A.[2]	06	New Hampshire, U.S.A.[2]	05
Indiana, U.S.A.[2]	06	New Jersey, U.S.A.[2]	05
Iowa, U.S.A.[2]	06	New Mexico, U.S.A.[2]	07
Jamaica	05	New York, U.S.A.[2]	05
Johnston Island	11	Nicaragua	06
Kansas[1], U.S.A.[2]	06	Niue Island	11 20
Kentucky[1], U.S.A[2]	06	North Carolina, U.S.A.[2]	05
Labrador[3]	03 30	North Dakota[1], U.S.A.[2]	06
Leeward Islands	04	Northwest Territories[3]	
Liberia	00H 44M 30s	(east of long. W 68°)	04
Louisiana, U.S.A.[2]	06	(long. W 68°–W 85°)	05
Low Archipelago	10	(long. W 85°–W 102°)	06
Madeira[3]	01	(long. W 102°–W 120°)	07
Maine, U.S.A.[2]	05	(west of long. W 120°)	08
Manitoba[3]	06	Nova Scotia[3]	04
Marquesas Islands[4]	10	Ohio, U.S.A.[2]	05
Martinique	04	Oklahoma, U.S.A.[2]	06
Maryland, U.S.A.[2]	05	Ontario[3]	
Massachusetts, U.S.A.[2]	05	(east of long. W 90°)	05
Mexico[5]	06	(west of long. W 90°)	06
Michigan[1], U.S.A.[2]	05	Oregon, U.S.A.[2]	08
Midway Islands	11	Panama Canal Zone	05
Minnesota, U.S.A.[2]	06	Panama (Republic of)	05
Miquelon	03	Paraguay	04
Mississippi, U.S.A.[2]	06	Pennsylvania, U.S.A.[2]	05
Missouri, U.S.A.[2]	06	Peru	05
Montana, U.S.A.[2]	07	Portuguese Guinea	01
Nebraska, U.S.A.[2]		Prince Edward Island[3]	04
(eastern part)	06	Puerto Rico	04
(western part)	07	Quebec[3] (east of long. W 68°)	04
Nevada, U.S.A.[2]	08	(west of long. W 68°)	05
New Brunswick[3]	04	Rarotonga	10 30

[1] This applies to the greater portion of the state.

[2] Summer (daylight-saving) time, one hour fast on the time given, is kept in some parts of the U.S.A., especially in the east and in the metropolitan areas. The dates of beginning and end are normally the last Sunday in April and the last Sunday in September or October, at 2h. 00m. local clock time.

[3] Summer time may be kept in these countries.

[4] This is legal standard time, but local mean time is generally used.

[5] Except the states of Sonora, Sinaloa, Nayarit, and the Southern District of Lower California which keep 7h.; and the Northern District of Lower California which keeps 8h.

	h. m.		h. m.
Rhode Island, U.S.A.[1]	05	Trinidad Is., S. Atlantic	02
St. Pierre and Miquelon	03	Trinidad	04
Salvador	06	Tuamotu Archipelago[3]	10
Samoa	11	Tubual Islands[3]	10
Saskatchewan[2]		Uruguay[4]	03
(south-eastern part)	06	Utah[2], U.S.A.[1]	07
(except south-eastern part)	07	Venezuela	04 30
Savage Island	11 20	Vermont, U.S.A.[1]	05
Scoresby Sound, Greenland	02	Virginia, U.S.A.[1]	05
Society Islands[3]	10	Washington, D.C., U.S.A.[1]	05
South Carolina, U.S.A.[1]	05	Washington, U.S.A.[1]	08
South Dakota, U.S.A.[1]		West Virginia, U.S.A.[1]	05
(eastern part)	06	Windward Islands	04
(western part)	07	(Grenada keeps summer	
South Georgia	02	time)	
Surinam (Dutch Guiana)	03 30	Wisconsin, U.S.A.[1]	06
Tennessee[2], U.S.A.[1]	06	Wyoming, U.S.A.[1]	07
Texas[2], U.S.A.[1]	06	Yukon	09
Tobago	04		

[1] Summer (daylight-saving) time, one hour fast on the time given, is kept in some parts of the U.S.A., especially in the east and in the metropolitan areas. The dates of beginning and end are normally the last Sunday in April and the last Sunday in September or October, at 2h. 00m. local clock time.

This applies to the greater portion of the state.

This is the legal standard time, but local mean time is generally used.

Summer time may be kept in these countries.

APPENDIX V

Table for Converting Degrees and Minutes of Longitude into Longitude Equivalent in Time

Example: Berlin, Long. 13° 24′E
Required Longitude Equivalent in Time

$$13° \quad = 0\text{h. } 52\text{m.}$$
$$24' \quad = \quad 1\text{m. } 36\text{s.}$$

$$13° \ 24' = 0\text{h. } 53\text{m. } 36\text{s.}$$

H M	°	H M	°	H M	°	H M	°
M S	'	M S	'	M S	'	M S	'
0 4	1	2 40	40	5 16	79	7 52	118
8	2	2 44	41	5 20	80	7 56	119
12	3	2 48	42	5 24	81	8 0	120
16	4	2 52	43	5 28	82	8 4	121
0 20	5	2 56	44	5 32	83	8 8	122
24	6	3 0	45	5 36	84	8 12	123
28	7	3 4	46	5 40	85	8 16	124
32	8	3 8	47	5 44	86	8 20	125
36	9	3 12	48	5 48	87	8 24	126
0 40	10	3 16	49	5 52	88	8 28	127
44	11	3 20	50	5 56	89	8 32	128
48	12	3 24	51	6 0	90	8 36	129
52	13	3 28	52	6 4	91	8 40	130
56	14	3 32	53	6 8	92	8 44	131
1 0	15	3 36	54	6 12	93	8 48	132
1 4	16	3 40	55	6 16	94	8 52	133
1 8	17	3 44	56	6 20	95	8 56	134
1 12	18	3 48	57	6 24	96	9 0	135
1 16	19	3 52	58	6 28	97	9 4	136
1 20	20	3 56	59	6 32	98	9 8	137
1 24	21	4 0	60	6 36	99	9 12	138
1 28	22	4 4	61	6 40	100	9 16	139
1 32	23	4 8	62	6 44	101	9 20	140
1 36	24	4 12	63	6 48	102	9 24	141
1 40	25	4 16	64	6 52	103	9 28	142
1 44	26	4 20	65	6 56	104	9 32	143
1 48	27	4 24	66	7 0	105	9 36	144
1 52	28	4 28	67	7 4	106	9 40	145
1 56	29	4 32	68	7 8	107	9 44	146
2 00	30	4 36	69	7 12	108	9 48	147
2 4	31	4 40	70	7 16	109	9 52	148
2 8	32	4 44	71	7 20	110	9 56	149
2 12	33	4 48	72	7 24	111	10 0	150
2 16	34	4 52	73	7 28	112	10 4	151
2 20	35	4 56	74	7 32	113	10 8	152
2 24	36	5 0	75	7 36	114	10 12	153
2 28	37	5 4	76	7 40	115	10 16	154
2 32	38	5 8	77	7 44	116	10 20	155
2 36	39	5 12	78	7 48	117	10 24	156

H M	°	H M	°	H M	°	H M	°
M S	'	M S	'	M S	'	M S	'
10 28	157	10 52	163	11 16	169	11 40	175
10 32	158	10 56	164	11 20	170	11 44	176
10 36	159	11 0	165	11 24	171	11 48	177
10 40	160	11 4	166	11 28	172	11 52	178
10 44	161	11 8	167	11 32	173	11 56	179
10 48	162	11 12	168	11 36	174	12 0	180

APPENDIX VI

PROPORTIONAL LOGARITHMS FOR FINDING THE PLANETS' PLACES

DEGREES OR HOURS

Min.	0	1	2	3	4	5	6	7	8	9	10	11	12	13	14	15	Min.
0	3.1584	1.3802	1.0792	9031	7781	6812	6021	5351	4771	4260	3802	3388	3010	2663	2341	2041	0
1	3.1584	1.3730	1.0756	9007	7763	6798	6009	5341	4762	4252	3795	3382	3004	2657	2336	2036	1
2	2.8573	1.3660	1.0720	8983	7745	6784	5997	5330	4753	4244	3788	3375	2998	2652	2330	2032	2
3	2.6812	1.3590	1.0685	8959	7728	6769	5985	5320	4744	4236	3780	3368	2992	2646	2325	2027	3
4	2.5563	1.3522	1.0649	8935	7710	6755	5973	5310	4735	4228	3773	3362	2986	2640	2320	2022	4
5	2.4594	1.3454	1.0614	8912	7692	6741	5961	5300	4726	4220	3766	3355	2980	2635	2315	2017	5
6	2.3802	1.3388	1.0580	8888	7674	6726	5949	5289	4717	4212	3759	3349	2974	2629	2310	2012	6
7	2.3133	1.3323	1.0546	8865	7657	6712	5937	5279	4708	4204	3752	3342	2968	2624	2305	2008	7
8	2.2553	1.3258	1.0511	8842	7639	6698	5925	5269	4699	4196	3745	3336	2962	2618	2300	2003	8
9	2.2041	1.3195	1.0478	8819	7622	6684	5913	5259	4690	4188	3737	3329	2956	2613	2295	1998	9
10	2.1584	1.3133	1.0444	8796	7604	6670	5902	5249	4682	4180	3730	3323	2950	2607	2289	1993	10
11	2.1170	1.3071	1.0411	8773	7587	6656	5890	5239	4673	4172	3723	3316	2944	2602	2284	1988	11
12	2.0792	1.3010	1.0378	8751	7570	6642	5878	5229	4664	4164	3716	3310	2938	2596	2279	1984	12
13	2.0444	1.2950	1.0345	8728	7552	6628	5866	5219	4655	4156	3709	3303	2933	2591	2274	1979	13
14	2.0122	1.2891	1.0313	8706	7535	6614	5855	5209	4646	4148	3702	3297	2927	2585	2269	1974	14
15	1.9823	1.2833	1.0280	8683	7518	6600	5843	5199	4638	4141	3695	3291	2921	2580	2264	1969	15
16	1.9542	1.2775	1.0248	8661	7501	6587	5832	5189	4629	4133	3688	3284	2915	2574	2259	1965	16
17	1.9279	1.2719	1.0216	8639	7484	6573	5820	5179	4620	4125	3681	3278	2909	2569	2254	1960	17
18	1.9031	1.2663	1.0185	8617	7467	6559	5809	5169	4611	4117	3674	3271	2903	2564	2249	1955	18
19	1.8796	1.2607	1.0153	8595	7451	6546	5797	5159	4603	4109	3667	3265	2897	2558	2244	1950	19
20	1.8573	1.2553	1.0122	8573	7434	6532	5786	5149	4594	4102	3660	3258	2891	2553	2239	1946	20
21	1.8361	1.2499	1.0091	8552	7417	6519	5774	5139	4585	4094	3653	3252	2885	2547	2234	1941	21
22	1.8159	1.2445	1.0061	8530	7401	6505	5763	5129	4577	4086	3646	3246	2880	2542	2229	1936	22
23	1.7966	1.2393	1.0030	8509	7384	6492	5752	5120	4568	4079	3639	3239	2874	2536	2223	1932	23
24	1.7781	1.2341	1.0000	8487	7368	6478	5740	5110	4559	4071	3632	3233	2868	2531	2218	1927	24
25	1.7604	1.2289	0.9970	8466	7351	6465	5729	5100	4551	4063	3625	3227	2862	2526	2213	1922	25
26	1.7434	1.2239	0.9940	8445	7335	6451	5718	5090	4542	4055	3618	3220	2856	2520	2208	1917	26
27	1.7270	1.2188	0.9910	8424	7318	6438	5706	5081	4534	4048	3611	3214	2850	2515	2203	1913	27
28	1.7112	1.2139	0.9881	8403	7302	6425	5695	5071	4525	4040	3604	3208	2845	2509	2198	1908	28
29	1.6960	1.2090	0.9852	8382	7286	6412	5684	5061	4516	4032	3597	3201	2839	2504	2193	1903	29
30	1.6812	1.2041	0.9823	8361	7270	6398	5673	5051	4508	4025	3590	3195	2833	2499	2188	1899	30
31	1.6670	1.1993	0.9794	8341	7254	6385	5662	5042	4499	4017	3583	3189	2827	2493	2183	1894	31
32	1.6532	1.1946	0.9765	8320	7238	6372	5651	5032	4491	4010	3576	3183	2821	2488	2178	1889	32
33	1.6398	1.1899	0.9737	8300	7222	6359	5640	5023	4482	4002	3570	3176	2816	2483	2173	1885	33
34	1.6269	1.1852	0.9708	8279	7206	6346	5629	5013	4474	3994	3563	3170	2810	2477	2168	1880	34
35	1.6143	1.1806	0.9680	8259	7190	6333	5618	5003	4466	3987	3556	3164	2804	2472	2164	1875	35
36	1.6021	1.1761	0.9652	8239	7174	6320	5607	4994	4457	3979	3549	3157	2798	2467	2159	1871	36
37	1.5902	1.1716	0.9625	8219	7159	6307	5596	4984	4449	3972	3542	3151	2793	2461	2154	1866	37
38	1.5786	1.1671	0.9597	8199	7143	6294	5585	4975	4440	3964	3535	3145	2787	2456	2149	1862	38
39	1.5673	1.1627	0.9570	8179	7128	6282	5574	4965	4432	3957	3529	3139	2781	2451	2144	1857	39
40	1.5563	1.1584	0.9542	8159	7112	6269	5563	4956	4424	3949	3522	3133	2775	2445	2139	1852	40
41	1.5456	1.1540	0.9515	8140	7097	6256	5552	4947	4415	3942	3515	3126	2770	2440	2134	1848	41
42	1.5351	1.1498	0.9488	8120	7081	6243	5541	4937	4407	3934	3508	3120	2764	2435	2129	1843	42
43	1.5249	1.1455	0.9462	8101	7066	6231	5531	4928	4399	3927	3501	3114	2758	2430	2124	1838	43
44	1.5149	1.1413	0.9435	8081	7050	6218	5520	4918	4390	3919	3495	3108	2753	2424	2119	1834	44
45	1.5051	1.1372	0.9409	8062	7035	6205	5509	4909	4382	3912	3488	3102	2747	2419	2114	1829	45
46	1.4956	1.1331	0.9383	8043	7020	6193	5498	4900	4374	3905	3481	3096	2741	2414	2109	1825	46
47	1.4863	1.1290	0.9356	8023	7005	6180	5488	4890	4365	3897	3475	3089	2736	2409	2104	1820	47
48	1.4771	1.1249	0.9330	8004	6990	6168	5477	4881	4357	3890	3468	3083	2730	2403	2099	1816	48
49	1.4682	1.1209	0.9305	7985	6975	6155	5466	4872	4349	3882	3461	3077	2724	2398	2095	1811	49
50	1.4594	1.1170	0.9279	7966	6960	6143	5456	4863	4341	3875	3454	3071	2719	2393	2090	1806	50
51	1.4508	1.1130	0.9254	7947	6945	6131	5445	4853	4333	3868	3448	3065	2713	2388	2085	1802	51
52	1.4424	1.1091	0.9228	7929	6930	6118	5435	4844	4324	3860	3441	3059	2707	2382	2080	1797	52
53	1.4341	1.1053	0.9203	7910	6915	6106	5424	4835	4316	3853	3434	3053	2702	2377	2075	1793	53
54	1.4260	1.1015	0.9178	7891	6900	6094	5414	4826	4308	3846	3428	3047	2696	2372	2070	1788	54
55	1.4180	1.0977	0.9153	7873	6885	6081	5403	4817	4300	3838	3421	3041	2691	2367	2065	1784	55
56	1.4102	1.0939	0.9128	7854	6871	6069	5393	4808	4292	3831	3415	3034	2685	2362	2061	1779	56
57	1.4025	1.0902	0.9104	7836	6856	6057	5382	4798	4284	3824	3408	3028	2679	2356	2056	1774	57
58	1.3949	1.0865	0.9079	7818	6841	6045	5372	4789	4276	3817	3401	3022	2674	2351	2051	1770	58
59	1.3875	1.0828	0.9055	7800	6827	6033	5361	4780	4268	3809	3395	3016	2668	2346	2046	1765	59
	0	1	2	3	4	5	6	7	8	9	10	11	12	13	14	15	

RULE:—Add proportional log. of planet's daily motion to log. of time from noon, and the sum will be the log. of the motion required. Add this to planet's place at noon, if time be p.m., but subtract if a.m., and the sum will be planet's true place. If Retrograde, subtract for p.m., but add for a.m.

What is the Long. of ☽ April 15th, 1970 at 2.15 p.m. ?
☽'s daily motion—11° 50'
Prop. Log. of 11° 50' ... ... .3071
Prop. Log. of 2h. 15m. 1.0280
☽'s motion in 2h. 15m.=1° 7' or Log. 1.3351
☽'s Long. on April 15th=15♌8+1° 7'=16♌15'
The Daily Motions of the Sun, Moon, Mars, Venus and Mercury will be found on pages 26 to 28.

INDEX